generalized anxiety disorder workbook

CBT Activities to Manage Anxiety, Cope with Uncertainty, and Overcome Stress

Lawrence E. Shapiro, PhD

Cover: Amy Rubenzer
Layout: Amy Rubenzer & Baker & Taylor Publisher Services

Disclaimer: This book is intended to be used as an adjunct to psychotherapy. If you are experiencing serious symptoms or problems in your life, seek the help of an experienced mental health professional.

ISBN 9781683734321 (print)
ISBN 9781683734338 (epub)
ISBN 9781683734345 (epdf)

PESI Publishing
pesipublishing.com

About the Author

Lawrence E. Shapiro, PhD, is a prolific author of self-help books and the inventor of more than 100 therapeutic games. Dr. Shapiro is known for his practical approach to helping others. He has written workbooks, storybooks, card games, board games, and smartphone apps. His work has been translated into 27 languages.

Table of Contents

Introduction

Is your life being taken over by your constant worrying? Do you find yourself worrying through the day about money, health, family, work, or other issues? Do you find it difficult to control your worrying even though you know it is not helping you? Do you expect the worst in almost any situation, even when you are aware that there is no real reason for concern?

If you answered yes to most of these questions, you likely have generalized anxiety disorder (GAD), a problem that affects over 3 percent of the US population. GAD is diagnosed when a person finds it difficult to control their worrying on more days than not for at least six months and has three or more of the following symptoms:

- Feeling nervous, irritable, or on edge
- Having a sense of impending danger, panic, or doom
- Having an increased heart rate
- Breathing rapidly (hyperventilation), sweating, and/or trembling
- Feeling weak or tired
- Having difficulty concentrating
- Having trouble sleeping
- Experiencing gastrointestinal problems

But you don't have to let your worries ruin your life! You can live your life in the moment. You can do things and go places whenever you want. You can live a fulfilling and happier life in just a few months—and this book can help. The four main sections provide worksheets to help you overcome your GAD. Although the exercises can be used on your own, we highly recommend you use this book with a qualified psychotherapist who can guide you.

The assignments can be thought of as therapy homework. Your therapist can explain why each exercise is important and also guide you in learning new emotional, cognitive, and behavioral skills that can stop your excessive worrying.

The Worry Paradox

If you are like most people with GAD, you have probably spent countless hours trying to find ways to stop worrying. You may try to talk yourself out of worrying, saying words like "My worrying doesn't help me" over and over again. You may try to distract yourself from worrying by binge-watching TV or doing something healthier, like exercising.

But these efforts to stop your worrying don't help, do they? If they did, you probably wouldn't be reading this book. In fact, studies have found that the more you try to stop worrying, the more you worry! This is what psychologists call the "worry paradox." You would think that trying to stop worrying would help you, but in fact, it often makes your worrying worse. This paradox is often illustrated by a simple experiment you might want to try right now.

For one minute, *don't* think about a giant pink elephant in your room.

If you are like most people, as soon as you try not to think about a pink elephant, it appears in your mind. And the harder you try not to think about it, the more likely that elephant is to be there.

Worries work the same way. The more you try to distract yourself from your worries, the more you tell yourself it is useless to worry, the more you try to fight your worries by replacing them with other thoughts, the more your worries will stick around.

So instead of trying to get rid of your worries, this workbook will help you understand your worries and accept them. And when you learn to accept them, you take away their power, and your worries stop being paramount in your life. Will you still worry sometimes? Of course. Everyone does. But this workbook can help you reduce your worries to a manageable level and give you the skills you need live a happy and fulfilling life without being tormented by constant anxiety.

What You Will Find in This Workbook

This workbook will take you through four main steps to overcoming your worries. Each step corresponds to a section of the workbook where you will learn specific skills on your journey to overcoming your anxiety disorder.

Section 1: Understanding Why You Worry and How It Affects You

The activities in this section will help you gain perspective on your worrying and how it affects your life, including the people you care about.

Section 2: Accepting Rather Than Fighting Your Worries

The techniques in this section will help you learn to tolerate worrisome thoughts and help you understand that thoughts are just thoughts and have no special power over you.

Section 3: Breaking the Habits That Keep You Anxious

You most likely have habits that support your worrying. The techniques in this section will help you recognize and change those habits.

Section 4: Developing New Positive Habits

This section will help you learn alternative habits that will help you live a more worry-free life.

Creating a Permanent Change

There is no right or wrong place to start in this workbook. All the techniques in it will be helpful. If you are in therapy for your anxiety, you should discuss where to start with your therapist or counselor, who may suggest specific techniques that will have the most immediate impact.

Learning new skills takes practice. Above all, it is important to be patient with yourself and persist in using these techniques even though they may be difficult at times. The treatment of anxiety, or any mental health problem for that matter, can quite literally change the way your brain works, but this can take some time.

I wish you the best in working to overcome your anxiety. If you are looking for additional resources, I recommend using the Anxiety and Depression Association of America website, which can be found at https://www.adaa.org/.

section 1

understanding why you worry and how it affects you

worksheet

Do You Worry Too Much?

Objective: To help you determine how your constant worrying is affecting your life.

You Should Know

Everyone worries sometimes. Thinking about the future, even when it makes you anxious, is a normal biological response to a perceived threat and a warning that you need to take action. However, you might worry all the time, so much that your excessive worrying interferes with your normal daily activities—robbing you of experiencing a full and happy life.

Excessive worry is often associated with depression and other emotional problems. It can be a significant stress in your life and can even contribute to physical problems. For some, excessive worry can also interfere with their relationships at home, at school, and even at work. If you constantly hear people say, "Why do you worry so much?" this may be a sign that your worrying has become a problem.

What to Do

Check off the statements that apply to you and write down at least one example for each statement you check.

_____ I constantly worry about something over and over again.

_____

_____

__X___ I notice that my muscles ache from so much tension.

_____my legs and shoulders_____

_____

_____

_____ My worrying makes me restless or antsy.

_____

_____

_____

X My worrying affects my relationships and social activities.

Don't seem to enjoy social activities like I use to

_____ My worrying affects my work or school performance.

X My family and friends are fed up with my worrying.

I'm constainly talking about my anxiety and asking questions about Cedar Hurst

X People tell me I worry too much.

Everyone tells me that they too have anxiety but have learned to control it.

X My worrying causes me to lose sleep.

I get enough sleep 8-12 AM awake then a light sleep is when I don't get up and get my mind on other good things

X I have a hard time concentrating because I worry so much.

this is why I forget things

X My worrying causes me to be irritable, and I take this out on others.

only my family not my neighbors

X I have several habits that I know don't make much sense, but they reduce my worrying.

walking up a down hall putting a warm heating pad

What is one aspect of your worrying that interferes with your life?

watch too much sports & news

What would be different in your life if you no longer worried so much?

I would be my old self, which was quiet fun, help others

What did you learn from this exercise?

To write down all my faults and work on them

What else can you do to make progress in this area?

Try harder to use the things Stacie gets me to help me relax a little

Are Your Worries Realistic?

Objective: To understand and accept that events are influenced by probability rather than your worries.

You Should Know

Just because something is possible does not mean it is probable. People with anxiety disorders are often consumed with the idea that something terrible will happen if they fail to act in a certain way. They become so overwhelmed by anxiety that they often do not take the time to realistically examine whether what they fear most is likely to come true. For example, it is *possible* you could be struck by lightning, but statistically it is *not probable*. It is also *possible* you could win the lottery, but statistically it is *not probable*. Anxiety disorders can make it difficult to distinguish between what is possible and what is probable.

What if you apply the theory of probability to your anxiety? Probability is the likelihood an event will occur. Of course, it is always possible your fears may be warranted, but is it probable? Most people with anxiety disorders imagine the worst outcome and act accordingly to prevent it. But think about this: If it is possible for the worst outcome to occur, it is equally possible for the best outcome to take place.

Consider Marcia's situation: Marcia was sure she would give a terrible presentation at work and feel embarrassed. She practiced giving the presentation to a friend, practiced in front of a mirror, and even took a video of herself and watched it again and again. Every time she practiced, she increased the probability she would give a good presentation.

What to Do

This exercise will help your rational mind better understand the concept of probability. You will begin by thinking of something you worry about because you think it could have a terrible outcome. Then you will look at nine other possible outcomes. With each outcome, you will consider the likelihood (probability) that the outcome will happen and why.

Begin by writing down the worst outcome you can imagine. Then write down other possible outcomes. Try to come up with nine other possible outcomes, *making sure at least three are positive ones.*

Now go back and write in the probability—low, medium, or high—that each outcome will occur and the reasons for your probability estimate.

Here are some examples from Marcia's worksheet:

Worry	Probability	Reason
I will make an idiot out of myself and get fired.	*Low*	*This is not probable because I spent more than 10 hours practicing the presentation. And besides, my work is really appreciated, so why would I be fired for screwing up a presentation?*
I will spill a glass of water on my presentation notes.	*Low*	*I'll take a sip of water before the presentation and won't even have a glass of water near where I am speaking.*
I'll get a standing ovation.	*Low*	*Even if I give a great presentation, the subject is not that exciting!*
People will be interested in what I say, and someone will give me a compliment.	*High*	*This is what happened the last time I gave a presentation.*
I'll have to go to the bathroom in the middle of the presentation.	*Low*	*This has never happened, and I'll use the bathroom before I start.*
I'll talk too softly, and someone will ask me to speak up.	*Medium*	*This has happened before, but it wasn't too bad and now I know I need to speak up a bit.*

Now try this for yourself.

Worry	Probability	Reason

Worry	Probability	Reason

Did you find yourself becoming anxious during this exercise? What thoughts came to mind when doing this exercise? Be specific.

_____

_____

_____

_____

_____

worksheet

Does Your Worrying Hurt You?

Objective: To identify the physical symptoms caused by your worrying.

You Should Know

The excessive worrying associated with GAD can cause you to have physical problems, just like any other form of stress. These common physical symptoms are associated with excessive worrying:

- Restlessness or feeling keyed up or on edge
- Being easily fatigued
- Muscle tension
- Dizziness
- Headaches
- Stomachaches
- Shortness of breath
- Dry mouth

Excessive worry is experienced by your body as stress, so your body reacts by producing stress hormones, including cortisol, adrenaline, norepinephrine, and others. An excess of these hormones is associated with high blood pressure, heart disease, a weakened immune system, and a variety of other serious illnesses.

Besides the direct physical problems that excessive worrying can cause, constant worrying can also lead to habits that cause poor health, including overeating or other dietary problems, sleep disturbances, and overuse of alcohol or drugs.

Note: *If you have ongoing physical symptoms, you should always see your doctor to find out if there is a medical cause to these problems and if these physical problems require treatment.*

What to Do

Begin by writing down the physical problems you think may be associated with your worry and anxiety. Note how often they occur: daily, weekly, or monthly. Next, rate the extent to which your physical symptoms are affected by your worrying, using a scale from 0 to 10, where 0 is "not at all affected by my worrying" and 10 is "always gets worse when I worry." Finally, add any comments regarding how worrying affects these physical problems.

Symptom	Frequency	Rating	Comments

Addressing the physical problems associated with your worrying requires an overall commitment to better health habits. It is important to understand that there is always a mind-body connection to your mental health problems, and working on your emotional *and* physical health will always result in the quickest improvement.

Following are four areas where you may be experiencing physical symptoms caused by your worry. Write down ways you could improve your physical health problems in each applicable area. If you anticipate having difficulty in making improvements in these areas, you may want to consult a health professional who specializes in that area.

Sleep

_____

_____

Exercise

_____

_____

Nutrition

_____

_____

Relaxation

_____

_____

How Do Your Worries Interfere with Your Life?

Objective: To understand how your worries keep you from doing the things that are important in your life.

You Should Know

Thinking about the future is different from worrying. Unlike other animals, humans have brains that are wired to think about the future. There is nothing wrong with thinking about what might happen in the future, as long as this thinking is based in reality and does not interfere with your ability to live life to the fullest and enjoy each day. However, if you find that excessive worrying is interfering with your life and causing you to be anxious, it is a problem you need to consider addressing.

Worrying can shape your whole life without your even realizing it. You might be so used to worrying all the time that you fail to realize how it is affecting your day-to-day choices. Sometimes you might even justify your worrying by saying that it shows you are concerned about others or it helps you focus on things that can be prevented. Again, it is okay to worry sometimes. But think about whether your excessive worry has become a habit you just take for granted. Has it become such a part of your life that you worry about even the smallest things throughout the day? Can you control your worrying, or does it prevent you from experiencing your life in the moment?

What to Do

Use the following worksheet for one week to try to catch yourself each time you think "What if…" and write down how this worry is keeping you from living your life to the fullest.

Example:

Your worry: *What if I ask for a raise and my boss laughs at me?*

How is your life being affected? *I might never get a raise if I don't ask for it, and I could really use the money.*

"What if..." Log

Week of _____

Worry	How Your Life Is Affected

Do you see a pattern to your worrying?

_____

_____

_____

What is something in your past you wish you had done but did not because you worried too much?

_____

_____

_____

Write down two things you would like to do that your worries are holding you back from.

1. _____

2. _____

Write down two things that could motivate you to try these things despite your worrying—for example, encouragement from a friend or the desire to do something fun with your family.

1. _____

2. _____

Understanding How Different Triggers Affect Your Anxiety

Objective: To identify the triggers that initiate and fuel your anxiety.

You Should Know

Many things can trigger worry and anxiety, and many of your worries may have several different triggers. Your worries might begin with an external situation or event, and anticipating this event triggers worrisome thoughts, memories, and physical sensations. These triggers can overlap and even seem like they are happening at the same time. When anxiety feels overwhelming, it might even trigger a panic attack, making it hard to recall how this episode started.

What to Do

Think about the last time you felt anxious as you complete this activity. The circles represent four different kinds of triggers. Write down what triggered your anxiety: an external event (e.g., giving a presentation), a thought (e.g., thinking about what might happen if you lose your job), a memory (e.g., recalling something from the past that made you anxious), and/or a physical sensation (e.g., feeling your heart racing).

You might discover that only two types of triggers are part of your anxiety, or you might see that all four types of triggers are involved. Make copies of the activity to fill out every time you feel anxious, and compare your triggers to see if there are any patterns.

My Anxiety Triggers

When you feel anxious, write down the triggers that seem to start and fuel your anxiety.

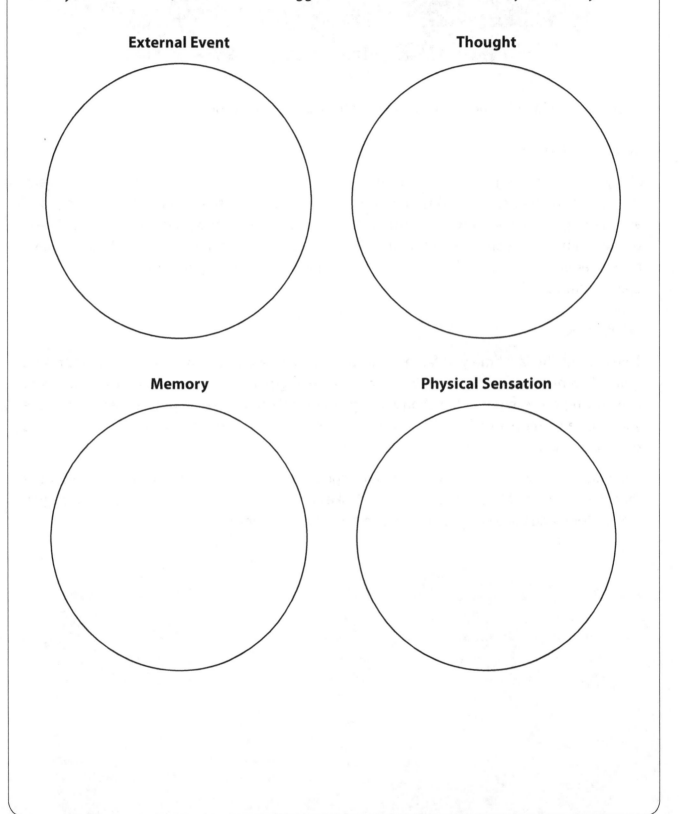

External Event

Thought

Memory

Physical Sensation

What was the most common thing that triggered your anxiety: an external event, a thought, a memory, or a physical sensation? Did you identify patterns? Why or why not?

_____

_____

_____

_____

_____

Did you try anything to stop your triggers from blending into one another? Describe what this process was like.

_____

_____

_____

_____

_____

How Does Your Worrying Affect Others?

Objective: To identify how your excessive worrying and anxiety is affecting those around you.

You Should Know

Most people with anxiety disorders cannot see how their constant worrying affects those around them because their worries are so prevalent and uncontrolled. If you find yourself worrying and anxious all the time, it is almost certain that your state of mind and your behaviors are affecting those around you.

The following are four common ways your anxiety can affect your relationships. Note that your anxiety can affect your relationships in different ways at different times.

1. You may be overly dependent. People with anxiety disorders often seek constant reassurance from those around them. They may want to hear that everything is going to be okay, and they may also require the physical presence of certain people in anxiety-provoking situations.

2. You may reject the company of others. Anxiety disorders can cause people to avoid certain social situations as well as certain people. Some people with anxiety disorders are ashamed of their constant worrying and associated fears and behaviors, so they find it easier to just be alone.

3. You may adopt a restricted lifestyle that also restricts those around you. Anxiety disorders typically cause people to lead restricted lives. This can be hard on the people around you who are constantly disappointed. People with anxiety disorders may avoid traveling, going to crowded places, or doing things that are unfamiliar. In general, people with anxiety disorders seek familiarity and avoid situations where there may be unwanted surprises. This cautious lifestyle will also affect those around you, who may limit their activities in order to keep you from getting upset.

4. You may turn to alcohol or drugs to calm your anxiety. It is common for people with anxiety disorders to self-medicate using drugs and alcohol. Obviously, this can present an entirely new set of problems that will affect those around you.

What to Do

This worksheet is designed to help you put yourself in other people's shoes and consider how your anxiety is affecting them. This exercise is not intended to make you feel guilty about your behavior, and it is certainly not intended to make you feel more anxious. Rather, it can help you better understand your anxiety disorder and hopefully motivate you to conquer your worries and fears, if not for your own well-being, then for the sake of others.

Fill in the names of significant people in your life who are affected by your anxiety. These could be relatives, friends, or coworkers. Then write down how your anxious behaviors affect each person. In the third column, you may wish to verify your thoughts with each person. You may find that you are correct about how others are affected, but you may also be wrong. It is entirely possible that many people close to you are unaware of your anxiety. Finally, write down anything you could do differently.

Person	How Your Anxiety Affects Them	Verification	What You Could Do Differently

Who in your life is most affected by your problems with worrying and anxiety? How are they affected?

_____

_____

_____

Is that person aware that you are trying to overcome your problems? _____

How do you think life will change for that person if you overcome your anxiety and excessive worrying? Be specific.

_____

_____

_____

What did you learn from this exercise?

_____

_____

_____

Keeping a Worry Log

Objective: To determine if there are any patterns to when you worry and what you worry about.

You Need to Know

According to a report from Johns Hopkins University, people who describe themselves as worriers can spend an average of 55 minutes a day worrying. Although this may seem like a lot, people with GAD spend an average of 300 minutes a day worrying—over five times as much. Most people who worry say they are thinking about the bad things that can happen regarding health, money, family, or work. People with GAD typically worry about little things as well as big things, such as:

- "Will I forget to put money in the parking meter and get a ticket?"
- "Will people show up late for my party and ruin the evening?"
- "Will my date hate the restaurant I chose and stop wanting to go out with me?"

Worrying all the time can be a tremendous psychological drain. Are you ready to worry less? Are you ready to have more time for your important relationships, your leisure activities, your work, and even ordinary daily tasks?

The first step to reducing your worrying is to understand it better, and you can do this by identifying the kinds of things you worry about, what triggers them, and how much anxiety they cause you.

What to Do

Make additional copies of the following chart and record your worries for a minimum of one week. Rate your anxiety from 1 to 10, with 1 being "a little anxiety" and 10 being "overwhelming anxiety."

Worry Log

Week of _____

Date/Time	Worry	Trigger	Anxiety Level

Did you notice any trends in the things you worried about throughout the week?

_____

_____

_____

Looking back, do you realize that some of the things you ranked highly maybe weren't as anxiety-inducing as you had expected? Why or why not?

_____

_____

_____

section 2

accepting rather than fighting your worries

worksheet

Observing and Accepting Your Worries

Objective: To begin managing your worries in healthier ways by observing and accepting them.

You Should Know

When you are worrying, it can feel impossible to think about anything else. You might seek out ways to avoid your worries or numb them with unhealthy or harmful behaviors. When you begin to recognize and accept your worries, you can identify healthier ways of managing your anxiety.

What to Do

When you are worrying, or your coping responses are causing even more anxiety, it is time to face those worries. The following visualization exercise will help you observe your worries, and any accompanying physical sensations, without analyzing them or becoming preoccupied by them. When you stop trying to fight or avoid your worries, the feelings become less intense, and it is easier to let them go.

Find a quiet, comfortable space to sit where you will not be disturbed or distracted, and set a timer for five minutes. As you become more comfortable sitting with your worries, you can set the timer for longer periods of time. Focus on your breath and your body's sensations throughout this exercise.

- Take several deep breaths and notice how your breath feels in your body.
- Notice your body's physical sensations, including any tightness in your neck or shoulders.
- Observe your worry as it arises. Describe the feeling to yourself, as well as the intensity of that worry.
- Notice whether the worry is increasing or decreasing in intensity as you continue your deep breathing.
- Observe any new worries that join or replace that worry.
- If you notice a need to push away the worry, or to act on a harmful urge, that is normal. Keep observing the worry a little longer.
- Observe how it feels to be aware of your worries, watching them come and go without acting on them.

- Remind yourself that worries are like waves that ebb and flow.
- Notice any judgments you have about yourself, other people, or the worry itself, and let them go.
- Keep watching your worry until it changes or decreases.
- Finish with a few intentional deep breaths.

Describe any physical sensations you noticed as you observed your worries.

_____

_____

_____

Describe any urges or impulses that arose as you observed your worries.

_____

_____

_____

Describe what it was like to observe your worries without acting on them.

_____

_____

_____

Did this exercise change the way you regard your worries? Why or why not?

_____

_____

_____

Did this exercise change the way you react to your worries? Why or why not?

_____

_____

_____

Can you think of ways to cope with your worries in the future?

_____

_____

_____

worksheet

Your Worries Are Just Thoughts

Objective: To understand that your worries are just thoughts and have no particular power.

You Should Know

Not all worries lead to anxiety. When people have so-called "normal" worries, they think of them as temporary concerns that can usually be solved pretty easily or that simply resolve themselves. These worries do not trigger physical reactions associated with fear. Normal worries don't keep coming back, and they don't affect your daily life.

However, people who worry excessively allow their worries to disrupt their lives. They typically think of their worries as real and something to be feared. They act as if they (or people they care about) are in real danger. But, in fact, there is no danger. People who worry all the time give their worries magical powers and forget they are just thoughts inside their head.

What to Do

This worksheet is intended to help you understand and accept that anxiety-provoking worries are just thoughts. Begin with the worry that troubles you the most. Then make copies of this worksheet for other worries that interfere with your life and cause you to be anxious.

Choose a frequent worry:

_____

_____

Say out loud: "This worry is just a thought."

How much do you believe this?

Rating _____ (where 1 is "I don't really believe this" and 10 is "I completely believe this")

Say out loud: "I am not in danger. No one else is in danger. There is no danger to confront."

How much do you believe this?

Rating _____ (where 1 is "I don't really believe this" and 10 is "I completely believe this")

Say out loud: "My anxiety makes my thoughts feel like they can really happen, but I know they can't. Therefore, I can't trust my feelings when dealing with my worries."

How much do you believe this?

Rating _____ (where 1 is "I don't really believe this" and 10 is "I completely believe this")

Say out loud: "I don't have to react to this worry. I can just observe it and let it go like I am watching a cloud drift away."

Close your eyes and imagine that your worrisome thought is just a cloud floating away. Breathe slowly and deeply as you let your thought drift away.

Describe how this exercise helped you understand that your worries are just thoughts.

_____

_____

_____

What did you learn from this exercise?

_____

_____

_____

Welcoming Mindfulness into Your Life

Objective: To bring mindfulness into your life by learning how to meditate.

You Should Know

Have you ever driven your car along a familiar route, going to school or work or to drop off your children at day care, only to arrive not remembering how you got there? Have you ever promised yourself just a few pretzels only to suddenly realize that somehow you ate the whole bag? This is what it means to be mindless—to travel though life on autopilot, never stopping to recognize what is really important to you.

Mindfulness means being aware of the thoughts, feelings, and physical sensations that are happening in your immediate environment. It means accepting all this information without judging it as right or wrong, good or bad. Being mindful allows you to function and grow along with the moment instead of flailing about in a past you cannot change or a future you cannot predict. People who are mindful take their time and allow themselves to appreciate every moment of their present.

You do not need to buy lots of fancy equipment or learn complicated words to meditate. You can sit, stand, or lie down, with or without a yoga mat or cushion. You just need to commit to a set amount of time every day. To introduce mindfulness meditation into your life:

- **Understand that your breath is important.** The focus is often on breath because the physical sensation of breathing is universal and natural to everyone. It is the center of life. Always come back to focusing on your breath, no matter what else your thoughts, emotions, and physical sensations tell you to do.

- **Know the goal is not relaxation.** Mindfulness meditation does not equal relaxation. The goal is not to escape or avoid your pain, but to observe it without attaching any meaning to it and move on from it by turning your attention to the present moment.

- **Return and repeat.** It is natural for your mind to wander at first. Simply recognize what is happening and return to your practice until you can focus for a longer period of time.

- **Be nice to yourself.** Avoid criticizing your abilities. This is not a contest, and you do not win or lose by being the best or the worst. You win by becoming one with yourself and leaning in to your world as it currently is.

What to Do

The 4-7-8 Method

This mindfulness meditation will help you focus on what is taking place around you instead of mindlessly rushing through life. It can help you better cope with the difficult thoughts and feelings that cause you stress and anxiety in your everyday life.

This practice suggests sitting because that is where many people feel most comfortable as a beginning step. However, you can also lie down. For best results, try to practice this exercise daily.

Sit restfully. Sit in a comfortable but firm chair that supports your arms and legs.

Observe your legs. Rest the bottoms of your feet on the floor. Feel the pressure of the floor pressing first against your heels and then your toes.

Straighten your upper body. Sit straight but naturally. Avoid forcing yourself into an unnatural position.

Observe your arms. Rest your hands and arms where they feel the most comfortable and stretch your hands out, feeling the stretch in each finger.

Rest your eyes. You can close your eyes, or if you do not feel comfortable doing that, simply allow them to wander where they want to without force.

Begin to breathe in and out.

- Inhale for four seconds through your nose.
- Hold your breath for seven seconds.
- Exhale through your mouth for eight seconds.
- Repeat this at least four times in a row.

When you are finished, slowly relax your focus and take a moment to notice your thoughts, your emotions, and any sounds in your environment.

How did it feel to integrate this mindful meditation into your life?

_____

_____

_____

How can you continue to bring more mindfulness into your life?

_____

_____

_____

worksheet

Calming Your Body with Progressive Muscle Relaxation

Objective: To reduce anxiety by learning and practicing progressive muscle relaxation.

You Should Know

Progressive muscle relaxation is a technique that involves tensing specific muscle groups and then relaxing them. We use the term "progressive" because you relax all the major muscle groups, starting with your head and working your way down to your feet, tensing and then relaxing them one at a time. In only 10 to 15 minutes, you can achieve total body relaxation.

This technique is particularly effective because it enables you to focus on your body tension. Although there are many other relaxation techniques that can help you reduce your anxiety, this technique may be most helpful for people who have body complaints that often accompany high levels of stress and anxiety, such as headaches, stomach problems, or muscle pain.

Relaxation techniques, such as progressive muscle relaxation, can be very effective in reducing anxiety, but only when practiced regularly. Engaging in an intentional relaxation practice for at least 10 minutes a day trains your brain and body to calm down on demand. As soon as you start to feel anxious, you can take a few deep breaths and think about how it feels to be calm, which automatically sends a message to your brain telling it to calm down, and to your body to release muscle tension.

Regularly practicing relaxation techniques not only helps you control your anxiety but may have other health benefits on the mind and body. For example, some research suggests that relaxation techniques can aid the body in the healing process and help in controlling high blood pressure and asthma, coping with chronic pain, and improving sleep problems. Many medical professionals also believe that daily relaxation exercises aid in preventing disease, reducing elevated levels of cortisol (the stress hormone), and bolstering the immune system.

What to Do

When you are ready to try this technique, find a place where you won't be disturbed or distracted for at least 15 minutes. You can use the following audio to help you learn this technique: https://www.betweensessions.com/wp-content/uploads/2021/10/BS_Calming_Your_Body_1-1.mp3. A transcript of the audio is also provided here.

In this exercise, you will travel up your entire body, from your feet to your head, bringing awareness to each muscle group—first tensing, then relaxing... tensing, and relaxing. As you tense your muscles, do not strain or exert yourself. Just notice the tension—gently squeezing, then harder, then hold, then release all the tension, letting go fully.

Find a comfortable, quiet place to sit or lie down, a place where you won't be interrupted and where you can relax completely. Turn off your phone. Lower the lights. You deserve this time—a time to calm your body and your mind. When you are ready, close your eyes.

Now allow yourself to come to a place of stillness, releasing any tension you are aware of. Let the floor or the seat support you fully.

Begin to notice the in-out rhythm of your breath. Notice your belly or chest rising and falling softly, as you gently inhale and exhale. In, out, in, out. No need to force or control your breathing. Just let it happen naturally.

When you are breathing in a steady rhythm, bring your attention to your feet and toes. Notice any tension. Now create more tension by gently scrunching your toes and contracting the soles of your feet. Now squeeze hard, as hard as you can without discomfort. Hold for a few seconds.

Now release. Breathe deeply, in and out. Notice the difference between the tension and relaxation. Enjoy the relaxation. Tense again. Now release. Notice the relaxation. Let go. Breathe.

Now bring your attention to your lower legs, your calf muscles. Notice any tension. Now create more tension by gently contracting the muscles in your lower legs. Now squeeze hard, as hard as you can without discomfort. Hold for a few seconds. Now release. Breathe deeply, in and out. Notice the difference between the tension and relaxation. Enjoy the relaxation. Tense again. Now release. Notice the relaxation. Let go. Breathe.

Now bring your attention to your thighs. Notice any tension. Now create more tension by gently contracting the muscles in your thighs. Now squeeze hard, as hard as you can without discomfort. Hold for a few seconds. Now release. Breathe deeply, in and out. Notice the difference between the tension and relaxation. Enjoy the relaxation. Tense again. Now release. Notice the relaxation. Let go. Breathe.

Now focus on the muscles in your buttocks. Again, notice any tension. Now create more tension by gently contracting the muscles in your buttocks. Now squeeze hard, as hard as you can without discomfort. Hold for a few seconds. Now release. Breathe deeply, in and out. Notice the difference between the tension and relaxation. Enjoy the relaxation. Tense again. Now release. Notice the relaxation. Let go. Breathe.

Next, bring your attention to the muscles in your abdomen. Once again, notice any tension. Now create more tension by gently contracting the muscles in your abdomen. Now squeeze hard, as if you're pushing your abdomen into the back of your chair or onto the surface of the floor. Squeeze as hard as you can without discomfort. Hold for a few seconds. Now release. Breathe deeply, in and out. Notice the difference between the tension and the relaxation. Enjoy the relaxation. Tense again. Now release. Notice the relaxation. Let go. Breathe.

Now focus on the muscles in your back. Notice any tension. Now create more tension by gently contracting the muscles in your back—now you might want to arch gently and tighten your back muscles as hard as you can without discomfort. Hold for a few seconds. Now release. Breathe deeply, in and out. Notice the difference between the tension and relaxation. Enjoy the relaxation. Tense again. Now release. Notice the relaxation. Let go. Breathe.

Now focus on the muscles in your shoulders and neck. Notice any tension. Now create more tension by gently contracting the muscles in your shoulders and neck, perhaps lifting them up toward your ears. Now squeeze hard, as hard as you can without discomfort. Hold for a few seconds. Now release. Breathe deeply, in and out. Notice the difference between the tension and relaxation. Enjoy the relaxation. Tense again. Now release. Notice the relaxation. Let go. Breathe.

Relax. Take a few more deep breaths and feel the weight of your body against the floor or chair. See if you can let go even a little more. Good.

Now focus on the muscles in your hands and wrists. Notice any tension. Now create more tension by gently contracting the muscles in your hands and wrists, curling them into loose fists. Now squeeze hard, as hard as you can without discomfort. Hold for a few seconds. Now release. Breathe deeply, in and out. Notice the difference between the tension and relaxation. Enjoy the relaxation.

Now open your hands and extend your wrists in the opposite direction, without hyperextending them. Now tense them hard as you can without discomfort. Hold for a few seconds. Now release. Breathe deeply, in and out. Notice the difference between the tension and relaxation. Enjoy the relaxation. Tense again. Now release. Notice the relaxation. Let go. Breathe.

Now focus on the muscles in your arms. Notice any tension. Now create more tension by gently contracting the muscles in your arms. Now squeeze hard, as hard as you can without discomfort. Hold for a few seconds. Now release. Breathe deeply, in and out. Notice the difference between the tension and relaxation. Enjoy the relaxation. Tense again. Now release. Notice the relaxation. Let go. Breathe.

Now focus on the muscles in your face, starting with your eyes. Notice any tension. Now create more tension by gently contracting the muscles around your eyes. Now squeeze hard, as hard as you can without discomfort. Hold for a few seconds. Now release. Breathe deeply, in and out. Notice the difference between the tension and relaxation. Enjoy the relaxation. Tense again. Now release. Notice the relaxation. Let go. Breathe.

Now bring your attention to the muscles in your lips and mouth. Notice any tension. Now create more tension by gently contracting the muscles of your lips and mouth. Now squeeze hard, as hard as you can without discomfort. Hold for a few seconds. Now release. Breathe deeply, in and out. Notice the difference between the tension and relaxation. Enjoy the relaxation. Tense again. Now release. Notice the relaxation. Let go. Breathe.

Now bring your attention to the muscles in your jaw. So many of us carry a lot of tension in our jaw. Notice any tension. Now create more tension by gently contracting the muscles of your jaw, from the mouth and position of the teeth to the hinge near the ears. Squeeze hard, as hard as you can without discomfort. Hold for a few seconds. Now release. Now open your mouth and stretch out your jaw completely, creating tension. Hold for a few seconds and release. Breathe deeply, in and out. Notice the difference between the tension and relaxation. Enjoy the relaxation. Tense again. Now release. Notice the relaxation. Let go. Breathe.

When you are ready, slowly come back to the present moment. Wake up your feet and hands, shaking them out if you wish. Wiggle your body and move around slowly at whatever pace is comfortable for you. Before you resume regular activity, take a few moments just to rest and breathe. You may use this recording at any time to help bring awareness to your muscles and to release tension in a safe, mindful way.

* * *

After listening to this recording a few times, you can practice this relaxation technique without the audio or script if you wish, but remember to relax for at least 10 minutes.

Make several copies of this chart, and keep a record of the time that you spend practicing this relaxation technique until it is truly a habit. You want it to become routine—something you do without thinking, like brushing your teeth. It is also useful to note your general mood, both before and after your daily relaxation exercise.

Day	Time	Mood Before	Mood After
Sunday			
Monday			
Tuesday			
Wednesday			
Thursday			
Friday			
Saturday			

Using Visual Metaphors to Accept Your Distressing Thoughts

Objective: To detach your anxiety from your distressing thoughts.

You Should Know

Many people spend a lot of time and energy trying to get rid of their distressing thoughts. Not so long ago, psychologists encouraged people to change their thoughts by making them more rational and reality oriented or to just suppress them entirely with techniques like snapping a rubber band on their wrists and saying "Stop!" in a loud voice. Although these techniques worked for some people, they tended to have only a temporary effect, and many found that their intrusive thoughts and worries would come back, often worse than before.

The newest approach to helping people who are overwhelmed by their distressing thoughts is to encourage people to stop trying to get rid of them at all! That may seem strange, because it is the opposite of what you feel like doing, and that is why therapists call it the "anxiety paradox." Therapists have discovered that the more you try to get rid of your thoughts, the harder it is to get rid of them. When you learn to accept your thoughts and detach from them, they will no longer have power over you.

The more you try not to think of something, the more it comes to mind. This is the paradox in action: The more you try to get rid of specific thoughts, images, and memories, the more they will take control of your mind and even your actions.

So stop struggling with your worries! Just accept them. Don't try to distract yourself. Don't try to change your thoughts. Certainly, don't try to dull your thoughts with drugs or alcohol. And don't pretend that your anxieties and worries don't exist.

Instead, as difficult as this sounds, just accept your worries, detach from them, and observe them without reacting to them in an emotional way. Try to objectify your worries, remembering that your thoughts are just thoughts; they have no special powers.

What to Do

This worksheet includes four metaphors that can help you understand and practice the principle of detaching from your worries by objectifying your thoughts and just observing them. After you read the different metaphors, practice using them several times a day. Even if you are not worrying at the time, you should still practice using these visual metaphors.

Don't Struggle in Quicksand

When you struggle to get out of quicksand, you sink in deeper. When you relax and float, you will eventually find that you are able to swim or walk out of the quicksand. Contrary to popular belief, quicksand does not suck you down. Quicksand is usually shallow, and when you stop struggling it is easy to get out.

Try using this metaphor to stop resisting your worries. Imagine that your worries are a pool of quicksand. Struggling against them will make it harder for you to get out. Accepting your worries as just thoughts and not real dangers will rob them of their power. When you stop struggling, your worries lose their power over you and you are able to just walk away.

After you do this exercise, rate your anxiety on a scale of 1 to 10, where 1 is "very anxious" and 10 is "very calm and disengaged from my worries": _____

Ignore Annoying Passengers in Your Car

You have probably had the experience of driving a car with annoying passengers. Maybe it is the kids making too much noise in the back seat. Maybe it is a friend or coworker sitting next to you who keeps complaining. What do you do? You just consciously tune out the noise from the passengers, letting it fade into the background, and you keep on driving. You don't stop the car, and you don't go in the wrong direction. You are aware of the annoyance, but you tune it out.

Now sit back and visualize yourself driving your car with your worries as the passengers. They are clamoring to get your attention, but you just tune them out. They are just background noise as you keep on going about your daily routine.

After you do this exercise, rate your anxiety from 1 to 10, where 1 is "very anxious" and 10 is "very calm and disengaged from my worries": _____

Watch the Worry Train

Imagine that your worries are on a train. Each boxcar contains a different worry. Visualize each car of the train, and then think for a moment about the worry that is in each car. Now sit back and visualize this train pulling out of the station. Watch as it rounds the bend and then continues on a journey out of sight.

Relax and visualize this metaphor.

After you do this exercise, rate your anxiety from 1 to 10, where 1 is "very anxious" and 10 is "very calm and disengaged from my worries": _____

See the Clouds Floating By

Think of something you are worried about. Say this worry out loud and visualize the worst thing that could happen. Now take a photo in your mind of that worry. Imagine that photo is resting on a cloud. Do not do anything to make the cloud go away, but just let it go where it wants. Watch it from the ground and see what happens to it.

After you do this exercise, rate your anxiety from 1 to 10, where 1 is "very anxious" and 10 is "very calm and disengaged from my worries": _____

After you have practiced using visual metaphors every day for one week, answer the following questions.

Have you noticed that you feel less anxious after a visualization exercise? Describe your feelings.

_____

_____

_____

How would you describe any changes in your mood during this week?

_____

_____

_____

Were there any changes in your behavior during the week?

_____

_____

_____

What did you learn from this exercise?

_____

_____

_____

Becoming Mindful of Your World Rather Than Your Anxious Thoughts

Objective: To draw your attention away from your anxious thoughts by using your five senses to focus on your surroundings.

You Should Know

Do you often find yourself agonizing over what might happen in the future, worrying about every possible thing that might go wrong, while simultaneously condemning yourself for what went wrong in the past? Being consumed by all this turmoil does not allow you to appreciate or enjoy the present moment.

Anxiety disorders can demand that you ignore what is taking place around you by bombarding you with disturbing thoughts, urges, and images. These unwanted experiences distract you from living your life in the moment and instead encourage you to obsess about a past you cannot change and an uncertain future you cannot predict or control.

What if you tried to live your life according to the uplifting and freeing principles of mindfulness instead of the rigid rules of your anxiety disorder? Mindfulness encourages you to notice and accept your thoughts without obsessing over them. By teaching you to focus on the present moment in a meaningful, nonjudgmental way, it takes the power away from your anxious thoughts.

What to Do

This exercise will encourage you to draw your attention away from your anxious thoughts and toward yourself, using your five senses as a guide.

- Commit to using your sense of sight, sound, touch, taste, and smell to channel your thoughts in a purposeful direction.
- Commit to doing this at least once a day for at least three weeks until you become accustomed to focusing your mind on the present.
- Begin by focusing on one sense for at least one to two minutes, taking the time to truly separate that sense from the next as you move from one to the other.

It does not matter what order you practice the five senses in. You can switch them around as you see fit. You can sit in a comfortable position the first few times, and as you become accustomed to the exercise, you can engage in it at any time or place.

At first this exercise may seem silly to you and even somewhat difficult, but as you continue to practice, you will find it easier to incorporate mindfulness into your daily experience until it becomes a natural part of who you are.

Five Senses Mindfulness Exercise

Sight

- Observe what is around you, noticing shapes, colors, and textures.
- Look for things you would not usually take the time to notice, such as shadows, a crack in the sidewalk, the texture of your bedspread, or any other small details that usually escape you.

Sound

- Take the time to listen to what is in the background instead of what is obvious.
- Don't just notice the sound of laughter, but try to discern different types of laughs.
- Rather than simply listening for the sounds of traffic, try to distinguish horns honking from tires squealing.
- Instead of becoming upset by loud music, take the time to figure out what genre you are hearing.
- Listen to previously unnoticed sounds, like the hum of the refrigerator or the clicking of the oven as it cycles on and off.

Touch

- Become aware of the differing feel of everyday items that surround you.
- Alternate touching items that are cold and warm, and notice how they make your hands feel.
- Touch items with various textures and notice the differences among them.
- Knit, play with modeling clay, or pet an animal, and feel the sensations in your fingers and hands as you feel the motions unfold.

Taste

- Take a drink, and notice the feel of the liquid rolling over your tongue.
- Chew on a piece of gum or candy, and take the time to notice the taste from when you first put it in your mouth until you are finished with it.

Smell

- Focus your attention on your surroundings to notice what different smells are in the air.
- Keep strong-smelling gum or candy with you to center yourself when you feel your anxiety rising.
- Items such as lavender, perfume, or lotion can also provide a satisfying aroma that invokes mindfulness.

Five Senses Meditation

For a five-day period, set aside at least 20 minutes per day to practice this meditation, focusing on a different sense each day. For each sense, choose one suggestion from the mindfulness exercise to focus on. Use the following chart to keep a record of your experience.

Sense	Focus	Observations	Feelings
Day 1			
Day 2			
Day 3			
Day 4			
Day 5			

After practicing mindfulness, what did you notice that you had not previously?

_____

_____

_____

Over time, how did practicing mindfulness impact your ability to focus on the present?

_____

_____

_____

What difficulties did you encounter in practicing your mindfulness exercises? What adjustments did you make, if any, to make it easier for you?

_____

_____

_____

How could you integrate the practice of mindfulness into coping with your anxiety disorder?

_____

_____

_____

worssheet

Taking a Noticing Walk

Objective: To bring awareness to the present moment by taking a walk outside and noticing your environment using all your senses.

You Should Know

One key component of mindfulness is being aware not just of what's going on inside you (thoughts, feelings) but also what's going on outside your body and mind.

These days, more and more people are walking around outdoors while looking down at their phones, whether it's at the beach, the lake, the mountains, or just around the neighborhood. We're connected all the time. Studies have even shown that looking at our phones constantly is changing our brains to be more active, seeking the next exciting stimulus, scrolling from thing to thing to thing, and never really stopping to notice.

Mindful walking in a beautiful environment is ideal for waking up the senses and noticing what's around us. We don't always have access to a beautiful environment, but taking a mindful walk in a noisy city environment can be a good exercise as well. In cold weather, you might choose to walk in a museum or library. The idea is to give yourself the experience of shifting your perspective outward, while remaining connected to your body, your thoughts, and your feelings.

What to Do

Go for a walk outside by yourself for a minimum of 15 to 20 minutes. Make sure to turn off your phone. Notice any sounds, really tuning in to everything you can hear—sounds up close, sounds at a medium distance, sounds far away. Take it all in. Notice what you feel in your body when you do this, without judgment and with acceptance.

As an alternative to a listening walk, you might choose to notice the smells in your environment. How many different smells can you notice? What smells pleasant (for example, a flower)? What smells unpleasant (for example, car exhaust, a skunk)? Notice what you feel in your body when you do this.

Noticing what you see is another type of mindful walk. Notice colors, shapes, sizes, and things that contrast. Look up to the sky. Look down at the ground. Take it all in consciously. Notice what you feel in your body when you do this.

If you experience some anxiety at being outdoors and opening up your senses, reassure yourself that nothing bad is happening. You could do a simple exercise that will help focus your mind and calm your body, such as identifying everything in your environment that is red, or green, or another color. Tell yourself everything will be okay. Or repeat self-compassionate statements as you walk. Congratulate yourself for trying.

When you get home, record the sounds, smells, and sights in as much detail as you can remember, and describe what it was like for you. Be creative. Do what feels good for you.

Location	Time	Observations	Feelings

Do you notice any difference in your mood after taking a mindful walk?

_____

_____

_____

Is this something you could do on a regular basis? Why or why not?

_____

_____

_____

How do you think this mindfulness exercise can help you deal with the current problems in your life?

_____

_____

_____

Tolerating and Overcoming the Physical Discomfort of Anxiety

Objective: To better tolerate and overcome uncomfortable feelings associated with anxiety by identifying and replicating them.

You Should Know

You might experience physical discomfort when you are fearful and anxious. If you think about a class or work presentation you have to deliver, your heart may beat faster, your chest could tighten, you may sweat, and you might even feel like you are going to faint.

These physical reactions can be scary, and you may feel like you are having a heart attack or are disconnected from reality. When this happens, you can become just as afraid of the physical reactions as you are of the actual situation that causes your anxiety.

One way to break this cycle of anxiety and fear is to intentionally experience the physical sensations that make you nervous and panicky. If this doesn't sound like fun, you're right—it isn't. However, studies indicate this is an important step in conquering anxiety.

What to Do

There are three parts to this exercise. The first part is to identify the physical sensations that accompany your anxiety. You will do this in the first column of the following chart. Circle the physical symptoms you have when you are anxious.

The next part of this exercise is to actually create those uncomfortable feelings. The second column will give you some ideas of how to do this. At first, practice these several times with a coach or friend in the room. This person will encourage you to perform the exercises so you mimic the physical sensations associated with your anxiety, and they will also protect you from any possible physical injury, like falling if you get dizzy.

The third and final part of this exercise is to record your practice recreating the physical discomfort that you associate with your fear and anxiety. Although this isn't pleasant, the more you practice, the sooner you will master your anxiety and lead a more fulfilling life.

The more you practice the physical feelings that you associate with anxiety and panic, the less likely you are to be negatively influenced by these feelings.

Uncomfortable Feelings	How to Create Those Feelings
Lightheadedness Feeling faint	Hyperventilate for one minute. Breathe loudly and rapidly (similar to a panting dog), at a rate of approximately 45 breaths per minute. Place your head between your legs for one minute, then quickly sit up.
Feeling weird or unreal	Think of how big the universe is and how small you are. Think about all your ancestors who have lived in the 200,000 years that humans have been on the earth. Sit in a completely dark and quiet room for five minutes.
Blurred vision	Stare at a light bulb for one minute and then attempt to read.
Difficulty breathing	Hold your nose and breathe through a straw for one minute.
Increased heart rate Tightness in your chest	Drink an espresso or other caffeinated drink. Do five minutes of moderately intensive cardiovascular exercise, like running up and down the stairs.
Upset stomach	Do 20 jumping jacks after a meal.
Feeling shaky	Tense all your muscles, and hold the tension for one minute.
Sweating	Wear a jacket or wrap yourself in a blanket in a hot room.
Feeling dizzy	Spin around really fast for one minute.

The saying "practice makes perfect" has never been truer than for people overcoming feelings of anxiety. Although it's not pleasant, practicing the uncomfortable feelings that accompany anxiety will help you control your emotions rather than having them control you. Use this chart to record the dates and times of your practice as well as your reactions. Rate your anxiety from each session from 0 to 10, where 0 is "no anxiety" and 10 is "extreme anxiety."

Date/Time	Physical Sensations	Emotional Reaction	Rating

Understanding What You Can Control in Your Life

Objective: To increase the sense of control you have in your life by identifying things you can control.

You Should Know

You might feel that you have little or no control over what happens to you, no matter how hard you work or how careful you are. Sometimes things go wrong in spite of your best efforts.

However, believing that all your experiences, both good and bad, are caused by luck or fate can lead to feelings of helplessness, hopelessness, anxiety, or depression.

What to Do

Rate the following statements, where 0 is "This does not apply to me at all" and 10 is "This always applies to me."

_____ I feel I have very little control over my life and what happens to me.

_____ I rarely get what I deserve.

_____ I avoid setting goals or making plans because too many bad things can happen along the way.

_____ I am often pressured into doing things or making decisions I later regret.

_____ Bad luck has caused many of the disappointments in my life.

_____ In spite of my hard work and effort, my accomplishments go unnoticed.

_____ Getting a good job depends mainly on being in the right place at the right time.

_____ I often feel hopeless and powerless about situations in my life.

_____ I make my decisions by flipping a coin.

Review the statements you checked off and add up your total score: _____

If your score is above 50, you probably feel you have little control in your life, and you might experience depression, anxiety, or feelings of hopelessness or helplessness.

Describe a time when you accomplished a task you set out to complete (for example, completing a creative project). What skills and strengths did you use to accomplish it? How did you feel about yourself afterward?

_____

_____

_____

Identify two small, achievable goals that are important or interesting to you. Include your desired date of completion. Then answer the questions that follow each goal.

For this example, Jim wants to improve his photography skills while meeting new people.

Goal #1: _____

Jim: To take an adult education class in photography by next April.

Steps I need to take to make this happen:

Jim: (1) Search online for local photography classes. (2) Visit my local camera shop for suggestions. (3) Determine how much tuition I want to pay. (4) Register for the class.

_____

_____

_____

_____

_____

The things I can control within those steps are:

Jim: All these things are under my control, except for the pricing and availability of the classes, but I will select which class I register for based on those factors.

_____

_____

_____

_____

_____

The strengths and skills I can use to address those steps are:

Jim: I will use my research skills to find a class that meets my needs. I will also use my organizational skills to create a list to track my class options and narrow down my choices.

_____

_____

_____

_____

_____

People and resources that can support me in achieving this goal are:

Jim: In addition to asking my camera shop for recommendations, I can reach out to my social media connections for suggestions.

_____

_____

_____

_____

_____

Goal #2: _____

Steps I need to take to make this happen:

_____

_____

_____

_____

_____

The things I can control within those steps are:

_____

_____

_____

_____

The strengths and skills I can use to address those steps are:

_____

_____

_____

_____

People and resources that can support me in achieving this goal are:

_____

_____

_____

_____

Of course, things do not always go as planned. When they don't, it is important to use self-compassion instead of beating yourself up or blaming other people or circumstances.

In the photography class example, it turned out that the registration was full, so Jim was unable to attend. Instead of saying "I'm so stupid for waiting too long to register," he can instead say, "I'm disappointed that I'm not able to attend the class in the spring, but I will register early for the summer class and add a reminder in my calendar."

Who can you count on for support and help if you are unable to meet a goal in spite of your best efforts?

_____

_____

_____

_____

_____

Did this exercise increase the sense of control you have in your life? Why or why not?

_____

_____

_____

_____

_____

Did this exercise change the way you see the role of luck and chance in your past successes or lack of success? Why or why not?

_____

_____

_____

_____

_____

Managing Catastrophic Thinking

Objective: To manage your catastrophic thinking by assessing the risk of your feared situation and identifying resources in the unlikely instance the situation happens.

You Should Know

Catastrophic thinking refers to ruminating about irrational, worst-case outcomes. It can increase anxiety, prevent you from taking action, or cause you to avoid situations entirely. When you fear the worst possible outcome, your choices, behaviors, emotions, and relationships can be negatively affected. You might constantly worry that something terrible will happen, and you might frequently experience "what if" thinking: "What if I catch a disease from visiting a sick friend in the hospital?" or "What if I lose my job?"

Fear can be a helpful reaction to situations where there are proven threats or dangers. It is important to know the difference between fear that is justified and based on evidence and fear that is based on catastrophic thinking or unjustified worries.

What to Do

Examples of catastrophic thinking and unproven fears:

- My house is going to get struck by lightning because I just replaced the roof.
- My spouse isn't answering his cell phone—he must have been in a car accident.
- I can't go on a cruise because the ship will sink.

Can you think of other examples from your own life? Describe them.

_____

_____

_____

Catastrophic thinking often causes people to avoid situations out of fear. Unfortunately, avoidance tends to reinforce this type of thinking—the more you avoid the fear-inducing situations, the more power you give them. The best way to conquer your anxiety is to examine the situation and determine the likelihood of that scenario happening.

Describe a recent situation you avoided because you were afraid something terrible would happen.

_____

_____

_____

Has that feared situation ever actually happened to you before? If so, describe that situation.

_____

_____

_____

Describe a time when your fears stopped you from taking action within your relationships, career, health, and so forth.

_____

_____

_____

Catastrophic thinking may relate to old beliefs and core values that produce overwhelming emotional reactions. You can examine your thoughts to determine how meaningful, accurate, and useful they are in the present situation. Challenging and changing those beliefs and values is often the key to managing persistent unhealthy or self-sabotaging thoughts.

In order to overcome catastrophic thinking, it is important to dispute the thoughts. You can:

1. Identify catastrophic thinking for what it is—an irrational, worst-case scenario. For example, you might imagine bad weather will destroy your home, even though it is simply a thunderstorm.

2. Determine best-case possibilities—the best possible outcomes you wish to see. The above-mentioned storm will not damage your home at all. You might just have to pick up a few downed branches once the storm is over.

3. Look at these best-case possibilities and identify whether they are the most likely outcomes. After checking the weather, you see the thunderstorm isn't expected to be severe enough to damage property.

4. Weigh the evidence and facts available to you so that you can develop a realistic contingency plan for coping with the situation. Once you check the weather and determine the storm will not be severe enough to damage your home, you feel a sense of relief.

Identify your feared situations and rank your level of fear from 0 to 10, where 0 is "no distress or discomfort" and 10 is "extreme upset or anxiety." Next, list the evidence that supports and refutes the possibility of the situation happening. Then describe a best-case possibility. Finally, estimate the odds of the worst-case scenario.

Feared Situation	Level of Fear	Evidence For	Evidence Against	Best-Case Scenario	Odds of Fear Happening

Did you notice any changes in your level of fear as a result of this exercise? Why or why not?

_____

_____

_____

What other steps can you take to cope with worst-case scenario thinking in the future?

_____

_____

_____

Tolerating Uncertainty

Objective: To expand the scope of your life by increasing your tolerance of uncertainty.

You Should Know

Uncertainty is an unavoidable part of life. No one can predict the future, so we must accept that there is some uncertainty in everyday life—and in particular situations there is a great deal of uncertainty.

Most people accept uncertainty as a natural part of life, but people with anxiety disorders often find it hard to accept uncertainty. For people who worry too much, uncertainty can act as a magnifier for their worries, feelings of anxiety, and even physical problems associated with stress.

Most people with anxiety disorders try to avoid situations that will increase their awareness of the uncertainty in life. They may avoid traveling, changing jobs, and even meeting new people. Some people avoid going to the doctor for a checkup because just making an appointment triggers their worry that something might be wrong with their health.

Avoiding situations that trigger your uncertainty will only diminish your opportunities in life. However, with practice, you can learn to accept aspects of life that are ambiguous or uncertain and cause you to worry unnecessarily.

What to Do

This worksheet is designed to teach you a simple process that can help you deal with uncertainty. The acronym **APPLES** will help you remember the mindfulness skills you need when you are uncomfortable with the unknown.

Acknowledge. Notice and simply observe uncertainty as it enters into your awareness.

Pause. Choose to respond, rather than react, to your experience. In fact, let go of the impulse to react altogether. Put your mind on "pause" and breathe calmly.

Pull back. Remind yourself that in this moment, it is fear, anxiety, or worry doing the talking. Thoughts and emotions are not facts. Notice that the need for certainty is not effective and is an impossible quest.

Let go. Give yourself permission to release yourself from the illusion that you must have certainty. No matter how intensely you believe you need certainty, remember that these thoughts and emotions are temporary and will pass.

Explore. Take a moment to explore your internal experience. Pay attention to your breathing and to all your senses. Observe the sensations around you: the sights, sounds, smells, tastes, and feelings. The emotional intensity associated with your distress will likely lessen as you do this. Now, choose to actively redirect your attention toward something other than your worries. Be present in your life.

Stand alone. When you are facing an uncertain situation that triggers your anxiety, do not ask anyone to go with you or try to keep in touch with people through calls or texting. Instead, face the situation on your own and use the following technique to cope without relying on others to reduce your anxiety.

The only way to learn to tolerate more uncertainty in your life is to put yourself into situations that would normally bother you and then see that being uncertain is not so bad. You can tolerate the thoughts and feelings that go along with uncertainty, and you can learn to live in the moment. You can use the **APPLES** technique to develop an attitude of acceptance, letting go, and paying attention to your thoughts and feelings rather than trying to avoid them. In the following chart, describe situations that commonly trigger your anxiety due to uncertainty. Rate how you feel, where 1 is "a little uncomfortable" and 10 is "extremely uncomfortable." Then choose at least one of these situations to practice the **APPLES** technique. See how many minutes you can spend each week tolerating uncertain situations, and then try to increase the time you spend tolerating these situations each week.

Situation	Rating	Date	Time Spent Practicing

Responding, Not Reacting, to Feelings

Objective: To manage difficult situations more skillfully by learning about the difference between reacting and responding.

You Should Know

Achieving good mental health means becoming familiar with and accepting all your feelings and not trying to escape or avoid them. Simply noticing your feelings, especially your unpleasant ones, without reacting to them can be a powerful skill in learning to deal with emotional problems.

The world is full of triggers that cause us to react rather than responding wisely: uncooperative, unsympathetic, or demanding people; events and situations beyond our control; disappointments and dashed expectations—they're everywhere! But it doesn't mean you should ignore your reactions; rather, you can learn ways to work with them.

When we respond, we stop, notice what we're feeling, assess the situation, and then decide what to do next in a thoughtful, wise manner. This definition is very similar to mindfulness—noticing what's happening in the present moment, without judgment and with acceptance. Then, mindfully, you can choose what to do next.

As with any new skill, you have to be willing to experience something new and unfamiliar. There will always be external events that bother us, but if we learn to respond and not react, we can make things better for ourselves, even if we can't change the world exactly to our liking.

What to Do

Once you are more familiar with your feelings, you can begin to notice where in your body you experience your feelings and what their intensity is. This will help you respond instead of reacting. Remember not to judge yourself harshly. Start with these steps:

- Take a deep breath. Better yet, take three breaths.
- Notice what you are feeling and where in your body you are feeling it (for example, jaw, neck, shoulders, chest, stomach).
- Note the intensity of the feeling (mild, moderate, strong).
- Let go of any tension you are aware of, to the best of your ability.

- Consider what is at stake—is it worth it to react with anger or impulsive action? What will the consequence(s) be?
- Respond to the person or situation with compassion, using clear, simple language.

For one week, note any incidents you might normally react to with frustration or anxiety, and see if you can respond to the incident in a positive way instead.

Sunday

Situation: _____

Reaction: _____

Feeling: _____ Intensity: _____

Where you felt it: _____

Response: _____

Outcome: _____

Monday

Situation: _____

Reaction: _____

Feeling: _____ Intensity: _____

Where you felt it: _____

Response: _____

Outcome: _____

Tuesday

Situation: _____

Reaction: _____

Feeling: _____ Intensity: _____

Where you felt it: _____

Response: _____

Outcome: _____

Wednesday

Situation: _____

Reaction: _____

Feeling: _____ Intensity: _____

Where you felt it: _____

Response: _____

Outcome: _____

Thursday

Situation: _____

Reaction: _____

Feeling: _____ Intensity: _____

Where you felt it: _____

Response: _____

Outcome: _____

Friday

Situation: _____

Reaction: _____

Feeling: _____ Intensity: _____

Where you felt it: _____

Response: _____

Outcome: _____

Saturday

Situation: _____

Reaction: _____

Feeling: _____ Intensity: _____

Where you felt it: _____

Response: _____

Outcome: _____

How did this exercise help you respond instead of react? Be specific.

_____

_____

_____

Five Steps to Deal with Intrusive Thoughts

Objective: To better handle recurring intrusive thoughts by accepting them rather than fighting them.

You Should Know

Everyone has unacceptable intrusive thoughts at some time. Take a look at these examples:

- Josh walked down the corridor of his school and suddenly had the thought that he might pull the fire alarm.
- Samantha stood near the edge of the rooftop of her building and suddenly thought she might jump off.
- Nadia was very religious, but while she was sitting in church, she suddenly felt like she might shout out some obscene words.

Most of the time, these are passing thoughts. Although they are totally unacceptable and may be completely out of character, they come and go very quickly, and minutes later people forget all about them. In many ways, they are more of a curiosity than a problem.

But for some people, intrusive thoughts get "stuck" in their brains. For example, a common intrusive thought of people with anxiety disorders is that something will happen to a family member and they will be hurt or even killed.

Unfortunately, the more you try to get rid of intrusive thoughts, the more they are sure to come back. Instead of trying to fight your intrusive thoughts, try to accept them. These five steps can help you do just that.

1. Label your intrusive thoughts as "just thoughts." Remind yourself that they have no power over you.
2. Tell yourself that these thoughts are just your brain going on autopilot and you can safely ignore them.
3. Accept and allow the thoughts into your mind. Don't try to push them away.
4. Breathe from your diaphragm until your anxiety starts to go down.
5. Continue whatever you were doing prior to the intrusive thought.

When you learn to accept your upsetting intrusive thoughts rather than fighting them, they will soon stop being a big part of your life.

What to Do

Forcing yourself to confront the upsetting thoughts you have been avoiding is the only way you can learn to accept them. This may seem strange, but the next thing you need to do is to *practice* having upsetting thoughts.

Write down situations that regularly trigger intrusive thoughts and what your most common thoughts are. Then, rate the distress you experience while having these thoughts, where 1 is "They hardly bother me" and 10 is "I can't stand them anymore." Practice the five-step acceptance procedure, then rate your distress again. Do this every day for at least two weeks and see if your intrusive thoughts are still playing a big part in your life.

Week of _____

Trigger	Intrusive Thoughts	Distress Level Before	Distress Level After

Did this exercise help you learn to accept your upsetting intrusive thoughts rather than fighting them? Why or why not?

_____

_____

_____

section 3

breaking the habits that keep you anxious

Using Coping Skills in Situations That Make You Anxious

Objective: To reduce your anxiety symptoms by identifying situations you avoid and learning techniques to cope with them.

You Should Know

You might believe that the best way to deal with your anxiety is to avoid situations that make you anxious in order to feel safe and comfortable. You might not want to feel fear or discomfort, but your desire for safety and comfort represents the biggest obstacle to overcoming anxiety.

To truly overcome anxiety, the first step is to accept the fear, face it, relax into it, and expose it for what it is—baseless and harmless. From a logical point of view, you may know that there is really nothing to fear. You may understand that you are not going to faint or have a heart attack, yet you still recoil in fear when you feel a twinge in your chest or experience lightheadedness. But until you actually experience the fear, face it, and learn that there is nothing to fear, it will be difficult to make lasting progress.

The steps to overcome anxiety include the following:

- Acceptance—Accept your fear and welcome it.
- Courage—Face the fear without running or avoiding the situations that make you anxious.
- Persistence—Repeatedly place yourself in situations that make you anxious.
- Patience—Allow time to pass so that your anxiety symptoms dissipate.

Many people deal with their anxiety by simply avoiding the situations that cause them to be fearful. While avoidance may reduce anxiety in the short term, it will also unnecessarily restrict your life and exacerbate your fears and worries in the long term. To conquer your fears and anxiety, you must learn to tolerate the situations that bother you, rather than avoiding them. This may seem difficult, but study after study tells us that this is the best way to rid yourself of anxiety.

There are many coping strategies you can use other than avoidance. Here are some of the most important in helping you cope with your anxiety.

Mindfulness: Mindfulness means paying attention to the present moment and not distracting yourself with other thoughts and activities. You can practice being mindful just by taking a walk and experiencing all of your senses as well as your feelings. Being mindful means accepting who you are at the present moment and not judging your experiences as "good" or "bad." When you practice mindfulness on a daily basis, it is easier to apply when you are anxious. Accepting your symptoms of anxiety, rather than trying to fight them, will make your anxiety feel much less powerful and put you back in control.

Diaphragmatic breathing: Also called belly breathing or deep breathing, this technique is one of the simplest ways to keep your anxiety from spiraling out of control. When you start feeling upset, try to find a quiet place to sit down and practice diaphragmatic breathing, even for five minutes. As the name suggests, diaphragmatic breathing means using the diaphragm muscle located just above your stomach. This type of breathing is easy to do. Put one hand on your stomach and the other on your chest. Breathe in through your nose for about three seconds as you feel your stomach expand, but let your chest remain relatively still. Purse your lips (as if drinking from a straw) and exhale slowly for about three seconds. You should feel your stomach flatten as you let your breath out.

There are several different apps that can help you with diaphragmatic breathing, including *iBreathe* and *The Breathing App*. These are available for both Apple and Android devices.

It's highly recommended that you practice this type of breathing for five to ten minutes every day, not just when you are feeling anxious.

Progressive muscle relaxation: There are many types of relaxation techniques, but progressive muscle relaxation is one of the most effective in reducing anxiety. Ideally, you should be reclining in a quiet place when you practice this technique, but it can help you cope with anxiety wherever you are. Progressive relaxation means consciously relaxing each part of your body, starting from the top of your head and moving to the tip of your toes. While in a seated position, relax the muscles in your face and head, proceeding down to your neck and shoulders, then to your torso and your hips, your legs, and finally your feet. As you consciously relax each area of your body, breathe deeply and try to clear your mind. Concentrate on how good it feels to let the tension out of your body and to enter a state of physical relaxation. Normally this exercise takes five to ten minutes and almost immediately reduces the brain chemicals that are associated with feelings of stress and anxiety.

Positive self-talk: Positive self-talk (also called affirmations) is just what it sounds like: saying encouraging things to yourself that will help you face your fears and worries. On a piece of paper, or in a note on your phone, write down positive statements to say to yourself when you are feeling anxious. Positive self-talk may seem a little weird at first, but it works! Many famous athletes and entertainers suffer from anxiety and use this technique to get past their anxious thoughts and perform at their best.

Visualization/imagery: Closing your eyes and imagining a peaceful, safe place is another way to deal with anxiety, and it is often combined with other coping techniques, like deep breathing or positive self-talk. When you start to feel like your worries and anxiety are taking over your mind, sit back and close your eyes, and imagine yourself lying on a quiet beach or taking a walk in the woods. Use your senses to help you create a vivid image in your mind. See if you can hear the sound of the waves breaking on the shore, smell the salty air, and even feel the gentle wind on your face. Your brain is very good at creating these multidimensional images based on your memory and your imagination.

Visualization can also be useful in practicing how to succeed in situations that make you anxious. You can use this technique to rehearse giving a speech, taking a test, or going to a social event you'd rather avoid. When you pair visualization with deep breathing and muscle relaxation, your brain gets the message: "This isn't so bad. I can get through this."

It is important to remember that as long as you do not feed your fear, symptoms will subside naturally, usually within minutes. Coping techniques are designed to break the fear cycle and to limit the duration and intensity of your symptoms.

Although some people mistake avoidance for coping, there is a difference between them. Coping skills must be used when you are in situations that cause you to be anxious, allowing symptoms to naturally run their course, without adding more fear to the process. Avoidance is a problem from a behavioral and learning standpoint because it does nothing to teach you that anxiety is not harmful, and it creates the false belief that you must try to escape from a situation to feel safe. Examples of avoidance behavior include running to be in the presence of a friend or "safe" person or fleeing to a "safe" place, like your car or a specific room in your home.

The only way to overcome anxiety is to experience symptoms without fleeing from them, avoiding them, or adding more fear to the situation. This means that you will experience times of extreme fear and discomfort. The good news is that if you are willing to do that a few times, it will begin to get easier very quickly. It doesn't take long for your courage to pay off as you suddenly find that you are no longer afraid of certain situations.

What to Do

The first step is to rank the situations you avoid because they make you anxious. Place a 1 next to the situation/place you avoid most often, a 2 by the situation/place you avoid next most often, and so on.

_____	Public speaking	_____	Auditoriums or stadiums
_____	Subways, buses, trains, airplanes	_____	Parties or other social gatherings
_____	Using a public restroom	_____	Crowds
_____	Walking on the street	_____	Restaurants
_____	Theaters	_____	Museums
_____	Shopping centers/malls	_____	Crowded elevators
_____	Dating	_____	Large rooms
_____	Standing in lines	_____	Other: _____

Now that you have identified the situations that make you anxious, choose one that you will practice experiencing over the next few weeks. Use this chart to keep a record of what happens.

Date	Situation	Coping Skill	Feeling and Reaction

Which strategies effectively helped you cope with your anxious symptoms?

_____

_____

_____

What else can you do to cope when you are in situations that make you anxious?

_____

_____

_____

How would like to approach this type of situation in the future after learning how coping skills can benefit you?

_____

_____

_____

Controlling Your Anxiety with a Worry Script

Objective: To face your negative thoughts and upsetting feelings by writing about them.

You Should Know

You might spend hours each day trying to avoid worrying about things that upset you. Do you distract yourself by checking your phone, playing video games, or even self-medicating with alcohol, drugs, or food? None of these things help reduce worrying.

In fact, the harder you try to avoid the thoughts that make you anxious, the worse they get. Trying to push something out of your mind is a little like trying to push a beach ball underwater: It takes a lot of work to keep it down, and the minute you let it go, it pops right back up again.

Rather than putting all your energy into avoiding upsetting thoughts and images, you can choose to face your fears, and writing worry scripts is one way to help you do this. By writing a script about your biggest worry, you will be facing your negative thoughts and upsetting feelings rather than trying to avoid them. Writing scripts will also help you get a clear picture of what is really upsetting you. Many people who write worry scripts for a few weeks report that they feel less anxious about the things they were worrying about.

What to Do

To write a worry script, choose a place where you won't be interrupted. Turn off your cell phone, music, and television. Set aside about 30 minutes to complete each script.

- Write about one thing you are worrying about.
- Write about the worst-case scenario of this worry.
- Write a script that is vivid and includes how your worry looks, sounds, and feels. Include your feelings and reactions.
- Write a new script on the same subject each day, going deeper into your feelings with each script.

After about two weeks, you can move to the next worry.

If you feel anxious or even tearful while you are writing, keep at it! Experiencing these feelings means you are on the right track. Even though it may be difficult, the more you face your fears and worries, the more likely they will eventually fade.

My Worry Script

Date: _____ Beginning time: _____ Ending time: _____

Summarize what you are worrying about in a sentence. _____

_____

Write about the worst-case scenario of this worry, making sure to describe your worry in vivid detail (e.g., what your worry sounds, looks, and feels like). Remember to write about the same worry for about two weeks before repeating this exercise with a new worry.

_____

_____

_____

_____

_____

_____

_____

_____

_____

_____

_____

_____

_____

_____

Eliminating Your Safety Behaviors

Objective: To cope with anxiety without depending on your safety behaviors.

You Should Know

Using safety behaviors to deal with your anxiety or other psychological problem may provide temporary relief, but in the long run it does not help. When you use safety behaviors, you choose to avoid your psychological pain rather than face it and accept it, likely prolonging your problems.

Do you use any of these common safety behaviors?

- **Disassociation.** When Trevor was feeling anxious before a meeting, he would pretend he was someone who was confident and assertive. However, as soon as the meeting started or someone mentioned his name, he found it hard to even breathe.

- **Denial.** Damian worried constantly about his health and would always think he had the worst disease possible. If he had even a slight headache, he would think he had a brain tumor. But if someone asked him whether something was wrong, he would just say, "No, I feel great" and keep his worries to himself.

- **Excessive information seeking.** Sharon was worried about her daughter being bullied in school, so she scoured the internet on a daily basis for information and called her daughter's teacher for an update several times a week.

- **Obsessive checking.** After Craig was robbed, he couldn't leave the house without checking that it was locked at least three times. Then he started checking to see if he locked his car, if he shut off his computer, and if he locked his office desk. He always needed to check things at least three times.

- **Rituals.** Carrie was always worried about taking a test. She felt that she had to wear the same clothes every time she took a test or she would fail. If she couldn't find the exact outfit she needed to wear, she would start to feel like she was having a panic attack.

- **Procrastination.** David was worried about getting his term paper done on time, but instead of just working on it, he would watch movies all evening and procrastinate until the next day. Whenever there was something he worried about, David just put off doing it.

- **List making.** Marcus made a list of everything he had to do each day and would check it constantly throughout the day. His list had every detail of his day—even brushing his teeth and taking a shower.

- **Excessive reassurance.** Elizabeth was planning her first trip abroad and kept thinking about all the things that could go wrong. She called her parents several times a day to talk about her fears and worries.
- **Impulsiveness.** Caleb had a difficult time asking women out for a date. However, if he met someone new at the office or at a bar, he would immediately ask her if she was single. None of the women he talked to seemed at all interested in him.
- **Doing everything yourself.** Every time Nora had people coming over to the house, she had to clean it completely. Her husband and her teenage children asked if they could help, but Nora was worried that they might not do a good job.
- **Doing everything for others.** Lauren was worried that her middle-school daughter was not going to get good grades, so she did many of her daughter's school assignments herself.
- **Self-medication.** Vanessa carried a small bottle of vodka in her purse and took a shot every time she had to ride in an elevator.
- **Indulging bad habits.** Tara worried that her boyfriend was seeing another woman, and the only thing that kept her from thinking about this was shopping.

What to Do

What are the two or three safety behaviors you use most? You can choose from the list or write in others you use.

_____

_____

_____

When have you recently used a safety behavior to deal with your anxiety or other problems? What was the situation, and what was the effect of the behavior?

_____

_____

_____

What do you think might have happened if you didn't use a safety behavior?

_____

_____

_____

Did you ever try to stop using one of these safety behaviors? What happened?

_____

_____

_____

For one week, write down each time you use a safety behavior to deal with your anxiety and what happened as a result of using the behavior.

Week of _____

Date	Situation	Safety Behavior	Effect

What would it take to give up your safety behaviors?

_____

_____

_____

What is the worst thing that would happen if you didn't use a safety behavior?

_____

_____

_____

Now that you understand how safety behaviors can actually keep you feeling anxious, you may be asking yourself, "How exactly do I give up the safety behaviors I've been using for a long time?" The answer is to replace the safety behaviors with coping techniques, like diaphragmatic breathing, positive self-talk, progressive muscle relaxation, and mindfulness. These coping techniques are explained in the activity Using Coping Skills in Situations That Make You Anxious.

It will be easier to replace your safety behaviors with coping techniques if you plan ahead and think about which coping skills are most likely to help you face your fears and tolerate your anxiety. Use the following chart to help you determine which coping techniques can replace your safety behaviors. Then, after trying out your plan, go back and rate your success on a scale of 1 to 10, where 1 is "not successful" and 10 is "very successful."

Safety Behavior	Replacement Coping Technique	How Successful Were You?	Comments

Giving Up Reassurance Seeking

Objective: To cope with your worries without seeking reassurance from yourself or others.

You Should Know

Many people with anxiety disorders constantly seek reassurance from others that things will be okay. Sometimes people seek reassurance from friends or loved ones. For example, Michael worried about his pregnant wife, even though she seemed to be having an easy pregnancy. He insisted that she call or text him every hour of the day when they were apart.

Other people seek reassurance from medical professionals. Paul had several panic attacks and thought he was having a heart attack. Each time, he insisted on going to the emergency room, even though his doctors had told him that there was nothing wrong with his heart.

Still others constantly read self-help books or search the internet for reassurance. For example, Annie Marie was recently divorced and was worried that she would never find anyone else to love. She had six books on finding love that she read over and over again.

In the past, many psychologists prescribed self-affirmations, a form of self-reassurance, as a way to cope with worries. They would have their patients say positive things to themselves in the mirror or carry around slips of paper with reassuring words written on them. Now we know that this type of self-reassurance will likely prolong your worries, just like seeking reassurance from others.

When you constantly seek reassurance, you are engaging with your worries as if they were real. It is much more helpful in the long run to recognize your worries for what they are and then just let them go.

What to Do

Answer the following questions, then complete the following exercise.

Is there someone you need to hear from every day? Is there more than one person? Write their names here.

_____

_____

_____

Are there people you always call when you are worried? List them.

_____

_____

_____

How do you think they feel about your need to hear from them?

_____

_____

_____

What are some things you seek reassurance about?

_____

_____

_____

What do you think will happen if you do not get the reassurance you need?

_____

_____

_____

Every time you feel you need reassurance about something that worries you, write it in the following chart. Then write down how would you like to get reassurance—but don't seek it! Instead, just think about your worry for a few minutes while breathing deeply. Let the thoughts and feelings associated with your need for reassurance float away. Then, after you have done this, rate your need for reassurance from 0 to 10, where 0 is "I don't really need reassurance anymore" and 10 is "I must have reassurance immediately."

Situation	Method of Reassurance	Rating

Make every effort you can to stop asking for reassurance about your worries. Tell the people you would turn to for reassurance that you are trying to change this habit. What might you say to them?

_____

_____

_____

Now think of all the free time you will have when you stop seeking reassurance for your worries. What are some positive things you could do for yourself with this extra time?

_____

_____

_____

What did you learn from this exercise?

_____

_____

_____

Using Imaginal Exposure to Reduce Your Anxiety

Objective: To decrease the control your fears have over you by indirectly exposing yourself to them.

You Should Know

You may be familiar with the therapeutic concept of directly confronting your fears in person. For example, if you were controlled by the fear that you may die from a spider bite, you could expose yourself to holding a spider in your hand. As an alternative, imaginal exposure therapy encourages you to indirectly confront your fears by using the strength of your mind.

What to Do

You will begin by creating a script where you write in graphic detail about a feared activity, situation, or object. Your goal is to become accustomed to interacting with your fears to the point where the debilitating anxiety you experience is diminished. You will achieve this goal by indirectly exposing yourself to your feared scenarios over and over again through reading or listening to your story until your anxiety dissipates. Although this may be the scariest thing you have ever done, remember that your fears and anxiety are only one small piece of you. The more important parts of you are what you value in life and the future you see yourself living.

You will follow these steps (which are explained in more detail next):

1. Choose one activity, event, or object that makes you anxious, and write a script about it.

2. Expose yourself to this script at least once every day for at least a week, or until your anxiety level goes down to 3 or lower on a scale of 1 to 10, where 1 is "no anxiety" and 10 is "overwhelming anxiety." Keep a record of your experience on the Imaginal Response Worksheet.

3. Answer the questions that follow the worksheet to reflect on your experience.

Write Your Script

Choose one activity, event, or object that makes you anxious, and write a detailed story about this fear. Be sure to include:

- Initial triggering event
- Physical sensations, including what you experience with your five senses
- Your thoughts
- Your actions
- Immediate consequences of your actions, including your feelings
- Long-term consequences you fear the most

Make sure to write in the first person and present tense, and see it through to the end, no matter how painful it is. Don't worry about grammar; this is for you, not for a writing class.

Finally, allow yourself to feel anxious. By allowing yourself to experience your fears and anxious feelings, you will eventually adjust to them, causing them to evaporate.

Before beginning your own script, read this sample:

Janine has started her first job as a fourth-grade teacher. Being recently out of college, she is worried about how the parents of her students will react to her. Every night she worries about the upcoming parent conferences. To face her anxiety, she writes a script describing her worst fears.

- Triggering event: I am meeting each student's parents for the first time to go over their student's progress. They look unhappy.
- Physical sensations: My heart is racing and I feel like I could faint. My mouth is dry and I'm worried about how I will sound.
- Thoughts: I'm thinking that these parents will be very critical and unhappy with me. They will blame me for any problems their child is having.
- Actions: I speak in a quiet voice and the dad keeps saying he can't hear me. The mom looks bored and sometimes looks at me like I don't know what I'm saying.
- Immediate consequences: I do a terrible job talking about this student. The parents are curt with me and seem very unhappy with the conference.
- Long-term consequences: Every parent conference goes poorly, and I keep losing confidence in my ability to teach. The principal schedules a meeting to talk about whether I should continue being a teacher.

Use this space to write your own imaginal script:

_____

_____

_____

_____

_____

_____

_____

_____

_____

Plan Your Imaginal Exposure

Commit to at least one session daily for a week. You have several options for the imaginal exposure:

- Read your script to yourself.
- Read it to a trusted friend or family member.
- Handwrite or type it over and over again.
- Record it and then listen to it in your car, on your phone, or on any other device.
- Copy it onto sticky notes that you can attach somewhere you will come in contact with them, such as your bathroom or bedroom mirror.

Do not rush! Take your time and remain in the situation until your anxiety level subsides.

Know that boredom is the opposite of anxiety and is therefore your friend. If you eventually get bored with your script instead of getting anxious, it means that you have conquered your fears.

And don't despair! If you find yourself feeling some anxiety even after you thought you were over this particular fear, re-expose yourself, beginning at the experience where you started feeling the anxiety again.

Imaginal Response Worksheet

First, write the date and the amount of time you spent on the exercise. Rate your anxiety level on a scale of 1 to 10, with 1 being "no anxiety" and 10 being "overwhelming anxiety," before and after the exercise. Add notes as needed, like emotions elicited or interesting observations. Record whether you met your goal of overcoming this feared situation.

Goal you would like to meet: _____

Date	Time	Anxiety Before	Anxiety After	Notes	Goal Met?

At the end of the week, write down your emotions, hesitations, ideas, progress made, or any other inner thoughts about your experience that you feel are important or necessary. Do this every week for the duration of your exposure therapy to track your progress.

_____

_____

_____

_____

_____

_____

_____

_____

Did this exercise reduce your anxiety? Why or why not? Be specific.

_____

_____

_____

_____

_____

_____

_____

_____

_____

You Don't Have to Be Perfect

Objective: To become more tolerant of the discomfort caused by embarrassing behavior by deliberately doing something that may be considered unusual.

You Should Know

Many people with anxiety have unrealistic expectations for themselves. They are tolerant of other people's flaws and gaffes, but not their own. Perfectionism can exist without anxiety, of course, but when the two are paired, it can be a crippling combination. Not only do people suffer from not reaching their own internal, self-imposed level of achievement, but they experience distress in a host of social situations based on an external measure of what they think they are *supposed* to be—perfect.

For example, at a choral concert, 60 choir members took the stage via a set of steps visible to the nearly 2,500 people on the expansive lawn at an outdoor venue. Marsha, who has a fear of making a fool of herself in public, stumbled on one of the steps and fell—*splat*—bracing herself with her hands. People helped her up, and she took her place in the lineup, but she was mortified. She was sure everyone in the choir and everyone in the audience was laughing at her and thinking she was a "stupid idiot." She continued to agonize about it throughout the concert and couldn't focus on her singing.

But here's the catch: It is likely that Marsha was the only one who even gave any thought to it after it happened, much less a critical thought. More likely, people felt empathy and hoped she was okay. This is how anxiety can interfere with one's life. But with awareness and practice, that can change.

What if you were to experience yourself as imperfect by embarrassing yourself *on purpose*? You might feel your anxiety rising at the mere thought of it. This form of exposure therapy is called *constructive embarrassment*. The idea is to expose yourself to uncomfortable feelings and learn to tolerate them—to actually welcome the feelings of embarrassment or humiliation—so you get used to them and realize nothing catastrophic happened and you're only human.

What to Do

On a scale of 1 to 5, with 1 being "least embarrassing" and 5 being "most embarrassing," rate the level of embarrassment you anticipate each of the following would cause. Then plan to do some of these socially feared things in public. You might want to invite an understanding friend or group of friends to practice your skills with.

Choose the activities that you rated as 1's and 2's at first, and gradually work your way up to trying a 4 or 5, but don't choose an activity that would cause you to have *extreme* anxiety. Afterward, record your reflections about the experience on the following lines.

Here are some possibilities. Feel free to add your own situations to the list.

_____ Stumble on purpose.

_____

_____

_____ Go to a movie after it has already started and ask to move past people who are already sitting.

_____

_____

_____ Jog in place in a park or at a bus stop.

_____

_____

_____ Make a phone call and then say you've got the wrong number and hang up.

_____

_____

_____ Knock over your glass of water at a nice restaurant.

_____

_____

_____ Dress casually for a formal event (or vice versa).

_____

_____

_____ Talk to yourself out loud at a supermarket.

_____

_____

_____ Face the wrong way in an elevator.

_____

_____

_____ Hum softly during a staff or group meeting.

_____

_____

_____ Appear in public with a speck of food on your face.

_____

_____

_____ Wear mismatched socks or shoes.

_____

_____

_____ At a meeting or in a class, ask a question that you're worried might make you appear stupid.

_____

_____

_____ Take an extra-long time at a stop sign.

_____

_____

_____ Do three separate transactions at an ATM while others wait.

_____

_____

_____ Skip instead of walking down the street.

_____

_____

_____ Pause for 10 seconds while giving a talk or speaking in public.

_____

_____

_____ Order a messy meal when you're on a date.

_____

_____

_____ Your own idea: _____

_____

_____

_____ Your own idea: _____

_____

_____

_____ Your own idea: _____

_____

_____

_____ Your own idea: _____

_____

_____

What is the worst thing that happened during any of these exercises? Did anyone make comments to you or look at you in a strange way?

_____

_____

_____

What thoughts did you have after you completed this exercise? Do you feel less anxious about the possibility of embarrassing yourself?

_____

_____

_____

Practicing doing the things you fear most is considered to be the best way to overcome your fear and anxiety. Do you think that you can continue this practice? Who can help support you in continuing to practice this kind of activity?

_____

_____

_____

section 4

developing new positive habits

Developing Self-Compassion

Objective: To become more compassionate toward yourself by envisioning an imaginary friend who loves and accepts you as you are.

You Should Know

You might have something about yourself that you do not like, something that causes you to feel ashamed, insecure, or not "good enough." Everyone does. Even people who seem to have everything—beauty, wealth, intelligence, and more—are often living with a sense of great inadequacy.

Do you think you are self-critical? Do you often feel that you are not as good as the people around you or that there is something really wrong with you? Ask yourself if you really need to suffer from your sense of not being "good enough." Suffering is part of the human experience, and we all will have times of pain, failure, and loss. But do you really have to add to your suffering?

Kristin Neff, a psychologist who has dedicated her life to teaching the importance of self-compassion, notes that self-compassion is not self-pity. She explains:

When individuals feel self-pity, they become immersed in their own problems and forget that others have similar problems. They ignore their interconnections with others and instead feel that they are the only ones in the world who are suffering.

Self-compassion is also very different from self-indulgence. Self-indulgence is merely giving yourself short-term pleasure, which may actually get in the way of your happiness and well-being. You may indulge yourself by eating a big bowl of ice cream, buying something special, or binge-watching your favorite show. These indulgences are fine once in a while, but they have little to do with self-compassion.

This worksheet is designed to help you bring self-compassion into your life. It will help you apply the same compassion to yourself that you show to those you care about very much.

What to Do

Begin by identifying something about yourself that you don't like. Write down one issue or thought that often makes you feel inadequate or bad about yourself, such as your physical appearance, a problem with your work, a relationship issue, or a mistake you made. Then continue with the rest of the exercise.

I feel bad about myself because:

_____

_____

_____

_____

What emotions come up for you when you think about this aspect of yourself? Write down as many emotions as you can.

_____

_____

_____

_____

Now take a moment to sit with these emotions even though they may make you uncomfortable. Just feel them without judging them. You might have some images or words come to mind. Don't judge them or try to get rid of them. Just observe them. *They are not you—only thoughts and images you have in your mind.*

Write down any images or words that come to mind.

_____

_____

_____

_____

Now that you are in touch with your self-critical thoughts and feelings, think about an imaginary friend who is unconditionally loving, accepting, kind, and compassionate. Imagine this friend can see all your strengths and weaknesses, including the aspects of yourself you wish you could hide from others.

Reflect on what this friend feels toward you and how they love and accept you exactly as you are, with all your very human imperfections. This friend has a profound understanding of what it means to be human. This friend is kind and forgiving toward you. This friend loves you unconditionally in spite of what you think of as your problems and faults.

In their great wisdom, this friend understands your life history and the millions of things that have happened in your life to create you as you are in this moment.

This friend understands that the things that make you feel bad about yourself are connected to many aspects of your life you didn't choose: your genes, your family history, the place where you were born, and many other things outside your control.

Write a letter to yourself from the perspective of this imaginary friend, focusing on the perceived inadequacies you tend to judge yourself for. What would this friend say to you about your flaws from the perspective of unlimited compassion?

_____

_____

_____

_____

_____

_____

_____

_____

In the words of this friend, express the deep compassion they feel for you, especially for the pain you feel when you judge yourself so harshly.

_____

_____

_____

_____

_____

_____

_____

_____

If you think this friend would suggest possible changes you could make, write them down. Make sure these suggestions embody feelings of unconditional understanding and compassion.

_____

_____

_____

_____

_____

_____

_____

Take a few minutes to feel this compassion. Feel the compassion from your imaginary friend as it soothes and comforts you. Sit back and close your eyes, and feel what it is like to experience unconditional love from someone who accepts you exactly as you are without dwelling for a moment on even the slightest critical thought.

Hold on to this feeling for another minute or two.

Now, imagine your friend wants to leave you with one important thought to carry with you. Just reading this one thought pours soothing compassion into you and comforts you like a cool breeze on a hot day or a warm blanket on a cold night.

Write down this one thought.

_____

_____

_____

Now, write down this thought again very slowly. With each word, see if you can feel the compassion and acceptance behind this thought.

_____

_____

_____

Grounding Techniques

Objective: To bring awareness to the present moment by learning and practicing grounding techniques.

You Should Know

Grounding techniques help people stay in the present moment during episodes of intense anxiety or other overwhelming emotions. Staying in the present moment allows them to feel safe and in control by focusing on the physical world and how they experience it.

Grounding is easy to do. Just pick an aspect of the physical world to focus on, rather than concentrating on your internal thoughts and feelings. Focus on the present rather than the past. Practice your grounding techniques so that they will come naturally to you when you are upset and want to let go of any negative feelings. Try a variety of techniques, and rate the effectiveness of each technique in keeping you calm. Have others help by reminding you to practice these techniques as soon as you are feeling emotionally distressed.

Here are some grounding technique suggestions. You can make up your own as well.

- Run cool water over your hands.
- Grab tightly onto your chair as hard as you can.
- Touch various objects around you, like a pen, your keys, your clothing, or the wall.
- Dig your heels into the floor, literally "grounding" them. Notice the tension centered in your heels as you do this. Remind yourself that you are connected to the ground.
- Carry a grounding object in your pocket to touch whenever you feel triggered.
- Notice your body: the weight of your body in the chair, the movement of your toes wiggling in your socks, the feel of your chair against your back.
- Stretch. Roll your head around.
- Clench and release your fists.
- Walk slowly; notice each footstep, saying "left" or "right" to yourself.
- Focus on your breathing, noticing each inhale and exhale.
- Eat something, describing the flavors to yourself.

Other ideas: _____

_____

Recording Your Progress

Begin by choosing five or more techniques you want to practice. Practice them several times a day for at least five minutes or until you feel calm and in control. Circle the number that best describes the effectiveness of each technique, where 0 is "no effect," 1 is "little effect," 2 is "effective but took time," 3 is "effective in keeping me calm and focused," and 4 is "immediate calming effect."

Technique	Date	Rating	Comments
		0 1 2 3 4	
		0 1 2 3 4	
		0 1 2 3 4	
		0 1 2 3 4	
		0 1 2 3 4	
		0 1 2 3 4	
		0 1 2 3 4	
		0 1 2 3 4	
		0 1 2 3 4	
		0 1 2 3 4	
		0 1 2 3 4	
		0 1 2 3 4	
		0 1 2 3 4	
		0 1 2 3 4	

Did this exercise allow you to become more aware of the present moment? Why or why not?

_____

_____

_____

_____

Did using grounding techniques reduce your anxiety? Why or why not?

_____

_____

_____

_____

Reducing Anxiety with Your Breathing

Objective: To interrupt the cycle of worry and anxiety by paying attention to your breathing.

You Should Know

Since the mid-1970s, when Herbert Benson, MD, researched and wrote about the "relaxation response," we have known that various relaxation techniques can reverse the brain's fight-or-flight reaction to fear and anxiety. The amygdala is the alarm center of the brain, and it gets triggered by even the slightest hint of danger, including worry. When it is triggered, it releases a variety of biochemicals that increase your blood pressure, heart rate, and muscle tension. This physical response is what most people refer to when they talk about their anxiety.

Deep breathing, along with other relaxation techniques, can help silence the alarm that triggers the amygdala and restore the body to a sense of calm. When you use deep breathing techniques, your body sends feedback to your brain, saying "All is okay; you can quiet down."

What to Do

Find a place where you will not be disturbed. Let people in your home know this is a time when you need to be alone. To get started, you may find it easier to lie on the floor. Use pillows under your head and knees for comfort.

- Place one hand on your lower abdomen.
- Breathe in deeply and slowly as you count to five, pulling your breath into your lower abdomen until it raises the hand that is resting there.
- Release your breath slowly and smoothly as you count to five.
- Focus on your breath as you do this exercise.

Once you have mastered the technique, you can do this without placing your hand on your abdomen. If you prefer not to lie on the floor, you can practice sitting in a chair as well.

Try to relax your body and your mind as you breathe. If you are distracted, simply bring your attention back to your breath. You may enjoy playing some soft, relaxing music or nature sounds.

This video from the Harvard School of Public Health shows Dr. Lilian Cheung demonstrating mindful breathing. Join the class! It takes just over 13 minutes. Link: http://youtu.be/8c-1Ylieg3g.

Once you get into the habit of deep breathing, you will find it easier to use this technique to calm yourself down when you start having thoughts that would normally make you feel anxious.

Here are three simple breathing exercises you can try this week. Choose which ones might be a good fit for you. Sit in a comfortable position in a chair or on a meditation cushion. Avoid slouching. In each case, if your mind starts generating a lot of thoughts, which it inevitably will, gently return to your breath.

In and out breathing. Set a timer for two minutes at first, then gradually work up to four or five minutes per sitting. Quiet your mind as best as you can and simply notice your breath going in and out. Don't push or strain or try to control your breathing in any way. Notice: Does the air enter through your nose? Your mouth? Just notice. Inhale. Exhale. Slow. Easy. No effort. Notice your chest or your belly rising and falling as you discover the rhythm and pace of your breathing.

Counting breaths. Sit comfortably and eliminate any distractions. Inhale slowly, counting up to five. One, two, three, four, five. Exhale slowly, counting down from five. Five, four, three, two, one. You may wish to hold for one or two counts before exhaling. Whatever counting pattern you choose, be sure not to strain or force your breathing. Easy, steady, in and out.

Belly breathing. Sit comfortably or lie down on a mat or soft carpet; avoid your bed, as you might fall asleep there. Put one hand on your belly and the other hand on your chest. Close your mouth and breathe in through your nose, deeply inhaling but not straining. Notice your belly rising, but keep your chest still. Exhale the air through your mouth, noticing your belly contracting slightly. Repeat up to 10 times.

Keep track of your progress on the following chart, noting the type of exercise, when and where you practiced, and for how long you practiced. Also note how it made you feel.

Type of Breathing	Time and Location	Length of Practice	How It Made You Feel

Did this practice reduce your anxiety? Why or why not? Describe your experience.

_____

_____

_____

_____

_____

_____

Embracing Your Worries with Humor

Objective: To reduce your anxiety through the use of humor.

You Should Know

Therapists tell us not to fight recurring and unwanted thoughts or worries, but rather to embrace them. It may sound strange, but research now suggests that the more you try to stop thinking about something, the more you *will* think about it.

Take a moment and give it a try. Close your eyes and visualize an alligator lying on your bed. Think about this image for a minute. Now try *not* to think about an alligator on your bed. For most of us, this is very difficult, and the image we are trying not to think about keeps popping into our mind.

What to Do

Write down something you worry about in one sentence.

_____

_____

_____

_____

Now take a look at the following humorous ways to deal with worries, and put a check mark by the ways you think you might like to try.

_____ Sing a song about your worry to the tune of "Happy Birthday" over and over again for five minutes.

_____ Draw a funny picture of the worst thing that could happen if your worry came true.

_____ Make up a story about something you worry about all the time, and add a terrible ending.

_____ Write down the thought you worry about 20 times. Now write it two more times with your nondominant hand.

_____ Translate your worry into another language. Now read the translation aloud five times. Now do it again in two more languages.

_____ Write down the thing you worry most about but reverse the order of the letters in each word.

_____ Get a plain T-shirt and write or draw your worry on it with marker. Make it as colorful as you can, and wear it around your home for a few hours. Don't forget to take a look at yourself in the mirror!

_____ Fill your mouth with food (try some crackers if you have them) and say the thought that worries you most five times.

_____ Imagine yourself worrying as if you were in a movie—a horror movie. Visualize yourself in the place where you are most likely to worry, except that a scary villain is playing you.

_____ Draw a comic strip about your worry or use an online comic-strip creator to make one up.

_____ Create a rap song about your worries and sing the song at least five times. If you want, you can share it with others.

Add your own ideas to help you embrace your worries with a humorous twist.

_____

_____

_____

Now for one week, try at least one humorous activity every day involving your most significant worry. Rate how you feel before and after each activity from 1 to 10, where 1 is "little or no anxiety" and 10 is "extreme anxiety."

Week of _____

Activity	Date/Time	Anxiety Level Before	Anxiety Level After

As you practiced different activities, did you notice any new thoughts? What were they?

_____

_____

_____

Did you find these activities humorous? Did you smile? Laugh out loud?

_____

_____

_____

Did you find that your anxiety around these worries diminished over the week?

_____

_____

_____

Did you share what you were doing with anyone else? What was their reaction?

_____

_____

_____

Practicing Self-Care and Self-Calming

Objective: To develop a more positive attitude toward life, to control your anxiety, and to feel more at peace by practicing self-care and self-calming.

You Should Know

You probably spend a significant amount of time every day doing things to ensure your physical health and prevent illness. But how much time do you take each day doing things to improve your mental health? Studies tell us self-calming practices contribute not only to better mental health, but also to better physical health, including improved circulation, a stronger immune system, increased pain tolerance, and more.

Self-care behaviors address your basic lifestyle. These habits have an almost immediate effect on your physical and mental well-being. They include:

- Getting at least a half hour of exercise each day
- Getting eight to nine hours of sleep each night
- Eating a well-balanced and nutritious diet, preferably low in sugar and food additives with multiple portions of fruits and vegetables each day
- Consuming alcohol and caffeine in moderation
- Spending time each day in the company of people who care about you

Self-calming techniques are planned and conscious behaviors that trigger your parasympathetic nervous system. These techniques slow your breathing, relax your muscles, and also lower your heart rate and blood pressure. Self-calming strategies simultaneously increase the brain chemicals associated with a positive mood and decrease those associated with stress. Self-calming techniques include:

- Progressive muscle relaxation
- Deep breathing
- Guided imagery
- Yoga
- Walking in nature
- Mindful meditation
- Massage

What to Do

This worksheet is designed to help you develop habits that are important to your mental *and* physical health.

Use this chart to keep track of your self-care and self-calming techniques for 21 days. Researchers tell us this is the amount of time it takes for behaviors to become habits. Rate your success in using these techniques on a scale from 0 to 10, where 0 is "My self-care was nonexistent" and 10 is "My self-care was excellent." Include the time you spent, the technique(s) you used, and what you can do to improve.

Day	Rating	Time Spent	Technique Used	Potential Improvements
1				
2				
3				
4				
5				
6				
7				
8				
9				
10				
11				
12				
13				
14				
15				
16				
17				
18				
19				
20				
21				

How did it feel to spend 21 days practicing self-care and self-calming techniques?

_____

_____

_____

_____

What else can you do to make progress in this area?

_____

_____

_____

_____

Filling Your Mind with Positive Thoughts

Objective: To reduce anxiety and develop a greater sense of well-being by thinking positively.

You Should Know

If you are troubled by anxious thoughts, it is important to accept them rather than fighting or avoiding them. You can tolerate anxious thoughts and understand they are just thoughts and cannot hurt you.

There is a four-step procedure to deal with these distressing thoughts:

1. Recognize and label your thoughts.
2. Observe them rather than reacting to them.
3. Replace anxious thoughts with positive affirmations or thoughts.
4. Allow time to pass.

Paying attention to positive thoughts can have many benefits, and continued practice may even help rewire your brain. Replacing anxious thoughts with positive thinking may actually help you cope better with stress, reduce your anxiety, and improve your health.

This worksheet is designed to help you determine if focusing on positive thoughts can help reduce your anxiety and improve your overall sense of well-being. It requires you to write down positive thoughts in a journal for two weeks and then reflect on whether this activity helped you focus less on your anxious thoughts.

What to Do

Get a journal or notebook, and each day for the next two weeks, pick at least one activity from the following list. Use one page for each activity. At the end of the two weeks, answer the questions about how this activity helped you and whether your anxiety was reduced.

Positive Thinking Activities

Activity	Date Completed
Write down five of your best qualities.	
Describe a favorite memory.	
Describe in detail the best day of your life.	
Make a list of your five most precious possessions.	
Make a bucket list of five things you would like to do.	
Write down five positive adjectives to describe yourself.	
Write down the names of five favorite people you have known.	
Write down five things you would like to do with your family.	
Write down five things you would like to do with your friends.	
Write down the names of five people who inspire you.	
Write down five things you are grateful for.	
Write about a dream place you would like to live.	
Write about a favorite role model and why you admire them.	
Write down something you are proud of.	
Describe a memorable birthday.	
Describe a favorite holiday and what you like about it.	
Describe a favorite place in nature.	
Write down a favorite dream you remember.	
Write down a favorite memory from your early childhood.	
Write down five things you are good at.	
Find and write down three inspirational quotes.	
Describe what you would do if you won $10 million in the lottery.	
Write down the names of five people you love.	
Write down the names of five people who have influenced you.	
Write down five things you have accomplished.	
Write down five good things that happened at school or work.	
Write down three vacations you would like to take.	
Write down the five funniest movies or TV shows you enjoy.	
Describe a favorite character from a book.	
Describe a favorite character from a movie.	
Write down any positive thoughts you are having today.	

At the end of the two weeks, answer the following questions.

Did you notice any change in your thoughts over the last two weeks? When did this happen? Describe your experience.

_____

_____

_____

_____

Ask someone who knows you well whether they noticed anything different about you in the last two weeks. Write down what they say.

_____

_____

_____

_____

Did you notice any decrease in your anxiety over the last two weeks? What else did you notice?

_____

_____

_____

_____

What was your favorite assignment out of all the activities you completed? Describe why it was your favorite and how it helped you.

_____

_____

_____

_____

Overcoming Anxiety with the Help of Exercise

Objective: To identify activities you can consistently engage in to decrease your anxiety.

You Should Know

Regular exercise can help you overcome your anxiety in a number of ways. During exercise, your brain increases the production of chemicals that can lift your mood and regulate your emotions. With regular exercise, you'll feel stronger and more confident, and be more likely to make positive changes in your life. Exercise will also increase the oxygen flow to your brain, which may help you think more clearly, rationally, and positively.

What to Do

Circle the types of exercise you can do on a regular basis.

Bike riding	Baseball	Football	Handball
Jogging	Hiking	Soccer	Karate or other martial arts
Walking	Skateboarding	Surfing	Pilates
Weightlifting	Basketball	Skiing	Yoga
Tennis	Swimming	Dancing	Golf

Write down other physical activities you think you can do that aren't listed.

_____

_____

_____

_____

To come up with an exercise plan, choose three exercises you would like to do over the next week. Decide how much time you need for each. 15 minutes? A half hour? An hour? Write down how often you can realistically do them in a week. Then write down which days are best to exercise and what time of day is most realistic.

Exercise	Time Needed	Frequency	Ideal Time

Once you have made a plan, use this chart to record how many times you actually exercise and the effect that exercise has on your anxiety.

Day	Exercise	Time	Mood Before	Mood After
Monday				
Tuesday				
Wednesday				
Thursday				
Friday				
Saturday				
Sunday				

After one week of consistent exercise, did you feel less anxious, more anxious, or about the same? _____

Describe your experience, including obstacles or challenges.

_____

_____

_____

How Diet Affects Your Anxiety

Objective: To improve your diet to decrease anxiety symptoms.

You Should Know

If you have anxiety, you may feel physically unwell. Coping with anxiety can be challenging, but making lifestyle changes may lessen your anxiety symptoms and make you feel better. Watching what you eat can help. Since diet, stress, and mood are all intertwined, it's important to consider what you're consuming—not only for your physical health but also for your emotional well-being. It's not necessary to go to extremes in changing your diet. By simply being more mindful of what you're putting into your body, you can find small ways to improve, and that can add up to big changes.

What you may want to avoid to lessen anxiety:

- **Caffeine.** This stimulant is in coffee, tea, chocolate, soda, energy drinks, and some over-the-counter medications. The temporary boost it provides can end in fatigue, headache, and tension. Caffeine is a potential trigger for anxiety attacks and a contributor to other health issues, such as insomnia, heartburn, aggression, irritability, heart palpitations, and high blood pressure.

- **Salt.** Sodium is present in many processed foods, so check labels and look for low-sodium or salt-free alternatives. Sodium consumption affects fluid retention, weight, and blood pressure, all of which can affect your mood.

- **Sugar.** Excessive intake of simple sugars (such as white or brown sugar and honey) can cause health problems such as hypoglycemia, which is often accompanied by symptoms similar to those experienced during a panic attack, and diabetes. Also, the temporary uplifting effects come with some other serious downsides, including an increased risk of depression in those who have a sugar-heavy diet.

- **Preservatives and hormones.** These substances are present in processed foods and many types of meats. Our bodies were not built to handle these additives, and their possible side effects have been heavily debated. Swapping in whole, unprocessed, organic foods can help reduce consumption of these potentially harmful substances.

- **Nicotine and alcohol.** Introducing these substances into your system can cause a range of problems—including aggravating anxiety. Nicotine is a stimulant, like caffeine, and alcohol is a depressant. Both can affect your sleep.

What can you eat to improve symptoms of anxiety? Try the following:

- **Eat a protein-rich breakfast.** You'll feel fuller longer, and your blood sugar will remain steady so that you have more energy.
- **Eat complex carbohydrates.** Carbohydrates increase the amount of serotonin in your brain, which is calming. Eat foods rich in complex carbohydrates, such as whole grains (for example, oatmeal, quinoa, and whole-grain breads or cereals).
- **Drink plenty of water.** Even mild dehydration can affect your mood.
- **Pay attention to food sensitivities.** Some foods or food additives can cause unpleasant physical reactions. These physical reactions may lead to irritability or anxiety.
- **Regularly eat healthy, balanced meals.** Nutritious foods are important for overall physical and mental health. Eat lots of fresh fruits and vegetables. It may also help to eat foods high in omega-3 fatty acids on a regular basis. Nutrient deficiencies can cause irritability, anxiety, and fatigue.

Note: *Changing your diet will make some difference to your general mood and well-being, but it's not necessarily a substitute for treatment. Lifestyle changes—such as improving sleep habits, increasing social support, using stress-reduction techniques, and getting regular exercise—will also help. If your anxiety is severe or interferes with your day-to-day activities or enjoyment of life, you may need counseling (psychotherapy), medication, or other treatment.*

What to Do

For the next month, keep track of what you consume, and describe how you feel each day. Rate your anxiety symptoms on a scale of 1 to 10, where 0 is "no anxiety" and 10 is "extreme anxiety." Make copies of the following chart, or use a notebook or diary.

Diet and Anxiety Log

Week of _____

Day	Food and Beverages	Substances	Anxiety Symptoms	Anxiety Level
Monday				
Tuesday				
Wednesday				
Thursday				
Friday				
Saturday				
Sunday				

After tracking your consumption for one month, describe your experiences. Did you have a decrease in anxiety symptoms? Why or why not?

_____

_____

_____

_____

Describe what you added or cut out this month. Did it make a difference, either increasing or decreasing your anxiety symptoms?

_____

_____

_____

_____

worksheet

Reducing Anxiety by Getting More Sleep

Objective: To improve your sleep habits in order to decrease anxiety symptoms.

You Should Know

Do you have a hard time falling or staying asleep? Anxiety causes sleep problems, and recent research indicates that a lack of sleep can aggravate anxiety. Sleep deprivation, common in anxiety disorders, may actually play a key role in stimulating brain regions that contribute to excessive worrying and may activate areas in the brain associated with emotional processing. Serotonin levels are impacted, affecting your mood. Getting enough sleep is an important part of your overall plan to overcome your anxiety and is also important for your general health.

There are a variety of techniques that can help you get the sleep you need, but, of course, they work only if you are diligent at trying them and then using the ones that are most effective. Here are some things you can try:

- Listen to soft music, read, take a warm shower, or meditate before going to bed.
- Exercise for at least 30 minutes each day, but not right before you go to bed.
- Write a to-do list for the following day, and then clear your head of those concerns.
- Practice deep breathing or progressive muscle relaxation before you fall asleep.
- Avoid caffeine, alcohol, and nicotine either entirely or at least in the evening.
- Keep your bedroom at a cool temperature, ranging anywhere from 60–65 degrees.
- If you are sensitive to light and sound, wear earplugs and a sleep mask, or try a white-noise machine to mask the sound. You can find a variety of white-noise apps online.
- If you have trouble falling asleep, get out of bed and do some light activity (like reading) in another room. Go back to bed when you feel drowsy.
- Go to bed and get up at the same time every day.
- Avoid eating heavy meals for at least two to three hours before bed.
- Make sure your mattress and pillows are comfortable.

What to Do

For two weeks, use the following chart to track your sleep and the methods you used to sleep better.

Sleep Tracking Chart

Date	Hours Slept	Sleep Quality	Methods Tried	Was It Successful?

What else can you do to sleep better?

_____

_____

_____

_____

Did the activities help you sleep better? Describe the two activities that helped you the most.

_____

_____

_____

_____

Did you face obstacles or challenges to falling asleep and staying asleep? Why or why not?

_____

_____

_____

_____

Preventing and Managing Lapses in Overcoming Your Anxiety

Objective: To identify early warning signs of a lapse so that you can respond appropriately.

You Should Know

As you start to successfully manage your anxiety, you will see that your symptoms begin to decrease or even disappear. However, you should know that at some point there may be a lapse—a temporary reappearance of symptoms. The more prepared you are for a lapse, the more likely it is that you will successfully get through it.

Lapses are common and can occur while you are still in therapy or months after you have finished your treatment. They tend to happen during times of high stress, when you loosen up on using your coping skills or start to make unhealthy choices. A lapse can also be a clue that you are going through a stressful situation that requires change.

What to Do

This worksheet will help you develop a plan to respond to a lapse now so you know what to do if and when it happens.

These tips can help prevent or manage a lapse:

- Be patient. Remember that change takes time and that a lapse does not mean you are back at square one.

- Do not avoid your anxiety. Be honest with yourself about your symptoms and what you are doing to cope with them.

- Reach out to someone if you need help. You do not have to suffer through anxiety alone.

- If you see symptoms creeping up, do not give up on yourself! A lapse can be discouraging, but you always have the choice to work through it.

- Do not mask your anxiety. Be careful of behaviors that temporarily give you comfort but limit your ability to make healthy choices, such as drinking alcohol. If you find yourself drinking more than usual, it may be a sign that you are masking some stress or anxiety.

- Live a balanced life. Managing anxiety is not just about coping skills. A healthy diet, restful sleep, exercise, hobbies, and leisure activities all contribute to an anxiety-free life.
- If you have been prescribed medication for your anxiety, keep taking it as prescribed. Talk with your doctor if you are thinking about stopping.

What are the people, places, thoughts, behaviors, or things that trigger your anxiety? In other words, what makes you anxious?

_____

_____

_____

_____

Write down the main symptoms you felt when you first began treatment. Try to be as specific as possible, because the longer you live without the symptoms of anxiety, the more difficult it may be to look back and remember how much they once impacted your life.

_____

_____

_____

_____

Write down the coping skills that you have found most helpful in decreasing your anxiety. Try to include details about why these skills have helped you or why you liked using them. You'll want to revisit these coping skills if a lapse comes up.

_____

_____

_____

_____

Keeping Track of How Medications Affect You

Many people decide to take medication to help with their anxiety. This is a decision you should make with your therapist and a physician with a knowledge of psychotropic medications. If you do decide to take medication, you might not experience immediate relief. In fact, while there have been many advances in psychopharmacology, finding the right medication to help you with your anxiety will almost always take some time.

There are different types of medications that help change the balance of chemicals that affect your emotions, and these are frequently taken in combination. It takes time and patience to determine exactly which combination of medications will work best for you. Unfortunately, there is no simple formula to guide physicians in giving you the exact medication to help you with your anxiety.

It is important to remember that psychological problems can also be a side effect of medications you take for other purposes. For example, drugs that treat high blood pressure can trigger anxiety. Always consult with your physician and pharmacist about the side effects of your prescription and nonprescription medication and ask how they interact and possibly affect your mood.

Keeping track of how you feel and function is really the only way for your prescribing physician to know which medications help your anxiety. Use this worksheet to keep track of your prescription and nonprescription medication, and bring it with you whenever you have an appointment with your doctor.

What medications or supplements do you take on a daily basis? Make sure to include the doses you take, as well as if and when the doses change.

Medication and Supplement Tracking Chart

Date	Medication	Time Taken	Side Effects	Mood